Praying Psalms

Praying Psalms

A Personal Journey through the Psalter

IAN STACKHOUSE

CASCADE *Books* · Eugene, Oregon

PRAYING PSALMS
A Personal Journey through the Psalter

Cascade Books
An Imprint of Wipf and Stock Publishers
199 W. 8th Ave., Suite 3
Eugene, OR 97401

www.wipfandstock.com

PAPERBACK ISBN: 978-1-5326-1842-0
HARDCOVER ISBN: 978-1-4982-4398-8
EBOOK ISBN: 978-1-4982-4397-1

Cataloguing-in-Publication data:

Names: Stackhouse, Ian.
Title: Praying Psalms : a personal journey through the Psalter / Ian Stackhouse.
Description: Eugene, OR: Cascade Books, 2018.
Identifiers: ISBN 978-1-5326-1842-0 (paperback) | ISBN 978-1-4982-4398-8 (hardcover) | ISBN 978-1-4982-4397-1 (ebook)
Subjects: LCSH: Bible. Psalms—Criticism, interpretation, etc. | Bible—Devotional use | Prayer—Christianity | Spiritual life—Christianity | Sacred books—Devotional use
Classification: BS617 S712 2018 (paperback) | BS617 (ebook)

Manufactured in the U.S.A.   08/28/18

In memory of the summer of 2014

In the last analysis, it is not so much what we get out of the Psalms that reward us, as what we put into them. If we really make them our prayer, really prefer them to other methods and expedients, in order to let God pray in us His own words, and if we sincerely desire above all to offer Him this particularly pure homage of our Christian faith, then indeed we will enter into the meaning of the Psalms, and they will become our favorite vocal prayers.

—Thomas Merton

Contents

Preface

THIS BOOK AROSE FROM a desire to express, in a series of brief impressions, the heart of the Psalms. Having prayed through the Psalter for over two decades, I wanted to capture in writing the genius of each psalm—at least from my experience of praying them. As it was, the practice of writing became itself a form of praying—perhaps the most profound form of praying.

Acknowledgments

I AM GREATLY INDEBTED, as in all things pastoral, to Eugene Peterson whose writings first introduced me about twenty years ago to the ancient practice of praying the Psalms. Since then, I have found numerous companions along the way who have shared a similar hankering for the kind of emotional expansiveness that the Psalter gifts us with.

I want to thank the Benedictine community of Douai Abbey, near Reading, who have given hospitality to me on various occasions and allowed me to participate in a liturgy simply laden with Psalms. Likewise, my thanks to the Dominican community of Blackfriars, Oxford, where I have been privileged, at the kind invitation of Timothy Radcliffe, to pray the morning office with the monks. And finally, in terms of religious orders, my thanks to the Monastic Fraternity of Jerusalem at St. Gervais in Paris. It was here that I first encountered the Psalms in French and truly wondered if I had arrived in heaven.

Closer to home, I wish to express my thanks to the Christian community I serve at Millmead who have been nothing but enthusiastic about my love for the Psalms, either in pastoral care, when the occasion arises, or in corporate worship. Indeed, at various times I have taught courses on the Psalms, and on one occasion put an evening together at Millmead in which I was able not only to reflect upon but also sing some of my favorite contemporary arrangements of the Psalms by Christian artists such as John Michael Talbot, Fernando Ortega, Michael Card, and the Sons of Korah. My deepest appreciation to Rebekah Duncalfe and her band for making that possible; and appreciation also, while I am thinking of Millmead, to the 6:45am Wednesday morning prayer group that I have met with for the last six years. Their faithfulness in prayer, compassion for the world, and love for the Psalms in particular, is one of the great joys of my life.

Finally, my thanks to my dear wife Susanna. The two decades that I have been praying the Psalms have coincided of course with our raising four sons who are just a complete delight to us. Whatever a quiver full is, I have enjoyed every minute of it. Now that they are grown up, may they also live a life immersed in the Psalms.

Introduction

I HAVE BEEN PRAYING the Psalms for a decade or so. In good monastic fashion, I start the first of the month with Psalms 1 to 5, end the month (on a thirty-day cycle, that is) with Psalms 146 to 150, only to repeat the whole thing again on the first of the next month. I haven't worked out how many cycles I have been through. The maths is pretty easy. But what I do know is that through repeated and sequential praying over so many years these psalms have become friends to me. As I hoped would happen, I have started to live a life shaped not only by the content of the Psalms but by their rhythm. There are days when I could tell you the time of the month simply by observing which psalms I am praying.

What provoked me to then write these reflections on the Psalms I can't quite recall. But beginning in the autumn of 2016 I started with Psalm 1 and each day, thereafter, "wintered" my way through the whole of the Psalter, concluding with Psalm 150 just one day before my fifty-third birthday. The idea was not to write a commentary, nor even to consult with a commentary,[1] but rather to write prayerfully, trying as best I could to get caught up in the heart of the psalm that was before me. Some days this was easier than others. And there were times when I most definitely veered from this spiritual discipline and started to think too much about what I was writing. But in the main what I have written here are succinct, immediate impressions of what I feel the Psalmist is saying, which will hopefully help those praying to orientate to the strange world of the Psalms. The reflections I offer are not meant to be prescriptive in any way, nor exhaustive of what could be said. How could they be? But if they can gently guide the reader into what is a fairly brutal regime of prayer, then I feel I will have done my job.

1. Although I must properly acknowledge Robert Alter's stunning translation of the Psalms: R. Alter, *The Book of Psalms: A Translation with Commentary* (New York: Norton, 2009), which was a constant companion as I wrote, as well as a new commentary on the Psalms by Walter Brueggemann and William H. Bellinger, Jr., *Psalms,* New Cambridge Bible Commentary (Cambridge: Cambridge University Press, 2014).

What struck me as I prayed these Psalms *seriatim*—one by one—was just how much pattern there was. Again, without going into a full-blown commentary, I became very aware over the five months or so of prayerful reflection that there was much more of an order to the Psalms than I had hitherto appreciated. Contrary to what might appear to be the case, these are no random collections of prayers but highly stylized books of prayers— five of them in fact—all with their own particular character. Some of the themes come out in my writing; some of it you will simply discover for yourself; and some of it you may want to consult with a more scholarly work in order to understand better the historical context. My point here is simply to alert the reader to a somewhat surprising order in the Psalms, and to have the courage to go with it. It's not that I have an aversion to categorization. The fact that some psalms are clearly laments, others psalms of thanksgiving, still others wisdom psalms, is a legitimate and at times helpful way of approaching the Psalter—and I acknowledge that at the top of each page by stating, courtesy of Brueggemann and Bellinger, the genre of each psalm. But don't let that hinder a more immediate and dare I say primitive response that comes by simply praying them as they are, and in the order they are given. A bit like when someone asks you how to read the Bible: start from Genesis and go all the way through to Revelation. How else are you supposed to read it?

For myself, I became aware through the experience of moving through the Psalms in sequence just how brutally honest they were. I had known this of course. Even a cursory reading of the Psalms will yield that data. But there were times over the winter when the candour of the Psalmist became overwhelming. With one or two interludes, it felt at times as if the whole of the Psalter was just one great outpouring of grief. Indeed, there were moments when even I wondered if the Psalmist had stepped over the line of what was permissible in terms of approaching God. Trying to ingratiate oneself with the Almighty is fair enough, but there were times when it felt like downright manipulation. On the other hand, I discovered this time round that what I had hitherto understood as vengeance—so called imprecatory prayer—was actually more of a cry for justice. I am not sure why I hadn't appreciated this before. I guess I had assumed that rawness meant revenge. But actually, as you pray those particular verses (sometimes whole psalms are imprecatory), maybe you too will feel, as I did, a greater coherence between the world of the Psalms and the world of the Gospels. Imprecations can feel very awkward to Christians. We are supposed to turn the other cheek, aren't we? But seeing them as a cry for justice helps us to see that maybe they are not as far removed from Christian ethics as we might think.

Which brings me to the person of Jesus. One of the things I have always been conscious of in my reading of the New Testament is just how many times the Psalms are quoted. In terms of what the scholars call intertextuality, you could almost say the New Testament is one long commentary on the Psalms. And where I became aware of this (actually, it is very hard as a preacher of the gospel not to be acutely aware of this), I decided not to ignore it but bring it into my reflections. I am a Christian after all, and although the Psalter is the preserve of other faith traditions, Judaism in particular, I felt it would be disingenuous of me to try to be other than I am. On the other hand, I have tried to ensure that these reflections on the person of Jesus end up not as pious devotionals but as personal and living discernments of the times when the world of the psalm and the story of the Gospels intersect, oftentimes in most astonishing ways. I guess you the reader will decide whether I have been successful or not.

As I say, this book emerged out of my daily prayers over the winter season. As with all my books, most of the writing was done between the hours of 5–7am. That's just the way it is for me. I have stopped apologizing for it. But of course, given the preponderance of references in the Psalter to the early morning, you can imagine that there were times when I was struck by the sheer poignancy of praying when the light in my own room was changing from what Yeats calls the "half-light" to the fullness of a new morning. It was worth getting up for. Indeed, I knew enough about the Psalms to know that this would likely happen to me as I went through the Psalter. I was not disappointed. What I hadn't accounted for, however (somewhat naively now I think about it), was the fact that I would be praying these psalms while life was happening to me. It was not a month or so into the project that I experienced a series of incidents which left me feeling incredibly bereft—perhaps more than I had ever felt before. Without going into all the details of what happened, suddenly the goal I had set myself of writing about each of the Psalms became less a spiritual discipline and more a matter of emotional therapy. In an uncanny way, the Psalms seemed to track my mood swings, but also, more importantly, offer me language that corresponded to the confusion, as well as the despair, I was feeling. Now that the storm has passed, I can better understand why Brueggemann talks about not only psalms of orientation and disorientation but also psalms of reorientation. This third category of psalms represent the return to some kind of normality, just like I have found, but not without the new perspective that the crisis has engendered.

In closing, my prayer is that this little primer on the Psalms will act as a source of renewal to those who obtain a copy. Whilst each entry has a few pertinent verses from the designated psalm, my hope is that the whole psalm will be read, followed by my reflection, which might then lead into another perhaps more prayerful reading of the psalm. My editor Robin Parry encouraged me to conclude with a short prayer of my own, which I have duly provided at the end of each psalm. It proved to be a very helpful way for me to conclude. But my hope is that praying the Psalms will elicit in you, the reader, prayers and reflections of your own, maybe even the odd journal here and there, and thus generate a whole raft of fresh thinking about this remarkable book of prayers that we call the Psalter.

This is not the first time I have written about the Psalms. In *The Day is Yours* I devote a short chapter to praying the Psalms.[2] And of all the more positive feedback I received about that book, it was that chapter on the Psalms that enjoyed the most acclaim. Even my father, who was never particularly lavish in his praise, enthused a great deal about it, to the extent that he requested that I send him a copy of the Psalms. What neither of us foresaw at the time was that this request became the prelude to us praying the Psalms together in the two months he came to live with us before he died. As I recall that time, it was the fact that he was having trouble sleeping that started it. I suggested to him one night, somewhat nervously, that instead of browsing on his iPad we might read a psalm together as the last thing before turning in. To my surprise, he agreed. He reckoned it to be a great idea. And so it was that each night I would choose a psalm, read it out loud, and then offer a brief prayer. Given that my father had not spoken of his faith for over twenty years, and had made it quite clear to me over the years that it was not up for discussion, you can imagine that these times with him were very precious. It was a gift that far exceeded anything I had hoped for. Hence, I would like to dedicate this book to the memory of those times, in the hope that this book will precipitate similar astonishing stories in the lives of those who read it and who pray the Psalms.

---

2. Ian Stackhouse, *The Day is Yours: Slow Spirituality in a Fast-Moving World* (Milton Keynes, UK: Paternoster, 2008), 91–97.

Book I

Psalm 1
Wisdom

¹ Blessed is the one
  who does not walk in step with the wicked
or stand in the way that sinners take
  or sit in the company of mockers,
² but whose delight is in the law of the LORD,
  and who meditates on his law day and night.

PSALM 1 IS THE entrance psalm. It presents us with a choice: whether to live substantially in God—like a tree planted by streams of water—or whether to live superficially with the world—like chaff flitting in the wind. One imagines the choice is easy, but it's not. And, of course, once you start walking in the counsel of the wicked it's not long before you find yourself standing with sinners, and not long again that you are sitting down in the seat of mockers. To put it crudely, it's not long before you find yourself in a rut, thinking and acting like any regular cynic.

Since the world has this kind of a pull, we must resolve to meditate our way into life: to leave behind the light confectionery of the world and chew on the meat of God's word. For sure, the rewards will not always be as clearcut as they are portrayed here. Life's circumstances can change very quickly. There will be psalms along the way to help us pray our questions about that. But for now, let us commit our way to God, rejecting the lightweight nature of our sound-bite world and delighting instead in the rushing rivers of a scripture-soaked faith.

Prayer: *Dear Lord, it is not always easy to choose for you. Broad is the road and wide is the gate that leads to destruction and there seem to be so many people on it. Help me to choose your narrow path, not to the detriment of my humanity but for the sake of its flourishing. Amen.*

Psalm 2

Royal

⁴ The One enthroned in heaven laughs;
  the Lord scoffs at them.
⁵ He rebukes them in his anger
  and terrifies them in his wrath, saying,
⁶ "I have installed my king
  on Zion, my holy mountain."

JUST IN CASE PSALM 1 has lulled us into a sense that faith is a very personal, private affair, Psalm 2 rudely awakens us to the political: to whole nations that are hostile to the God we have come to adore. Here we are meditating on his law; here they are plotting against the Lord and his anointed one. Everywhere you look, people are casting off restraint, seeking one way or another to come out from under the obvious and universal scope of God's rule. Turn on the radio first thing in the morning to hear the news and you wonder if there is a God at all, such is the posturing of those in power.

How ridiculous this all seems to the Lord. The One enthroned in heaven laughs. And as with all laughter, suddenly we get things back into perspective: that what lies at the heart of all things is not the noise emanating from a power-obsessed media but the quietness of a modest little mountain, in a tiny little kingdom, in a backwater of the world's greatest empire. Here on God's holy hill the language is not rasping but intimate. The Father loves the Son and has placed all things in his hands (John 3:35). The Son likewise, in filial reverence, calls upon the Father to make it so.

Prayer: *Dear Lord, it scares me that you are willing to dash the nations to pieces like pottery. You are not a safe God. But I am glad that you are the King and that you are good. Amen.*

Psalm 3
Individual Lament

³ But you, LORD, are a shield around me,
  my glory, the One who lifts my head high.
⁴ I call out to the LORD,
  and he answers me from his holy mountain.

I LOVE THESE PSALMS. Nothing abstract. Nothing academic. Rather, a storied universe. And no sadder story than David fleeing from Absalom his son. As we take up this exquisite psalm, one can almost see David, barefoot and head covered in mourning (2 Sam 15:30), crossing the Kidron Valley, up the Mount of Olives, not knowing if he would ever see the city again. In fact, he is not entirely sure if this is not the judgment of God upon him. Shimei certainly thinks it is and starts pelting the downcast Majesty with stones (2 Sam 16:8).

For as many times as I have read this story I have always wondered why David did not retaliate. Goodness knows, his troops were willing. David kept walking on, however, showered in the dirt of his enemies' curses. I guess the reason he didn't fight is because he prayed. And in this prayer he remembers that when we are bowed down in shame, surrounded by naysayers, God shows his kindest heart by putting his finger under our chin, lifting up our heads, and giving us a touch of glory—enough to sustain us through the long barren months. Such is the power of his touch, the surround of his shield, that we will not lose one night's sleep.

Prayer: *Many times, dear Lord, I feel I am walking away with my head bowed down. I feel hurt by the injustice. But I thank you that your love is bigger than my anger and your glory bigger than my shame. Amen.*

Psalm 4
Individual Lament

⁶ Many, Lord, are asking, "Who will bring us prosperity?"
  Let the light of your face shine on us.
⁷ Fill my heart with joy
  when their grain and new wine abound.

HAVE YOU NOTICED THAT we are not four psalms in and already two of them express deep cries of anguish? A good third of the Psalter is taken up with similar laments. It is striking to me that modern worship songs, by way of comparison, contain little or no lament. It suggests that the world is much more benign these days or, more likely, that somehow we have found ways to cocoon ourselves from the tough questions. Real faith, however, refuses to indulge itself like this. Real faith tackles reality head on. It begs the question "why?" and "what?" and "how long?" It wrestles with the gap between promise and fulfillment. Without in any way falling into self-righteousness, it weeps over the lack of seriousness in the land, and mourns that so many seem enamoured by vanity and lies. Amidst a culture that seems to be amusing itself to death, real faith counsels the searching of one's soul, a vow of silence, and the restoration of trust. It also holds on to the conviction that the hallmark of a religious life is not sour-faced sanctimoniousness—God forbid—but intoxicating joy. What better advert for a life in God than a people drunk on the new wine of the kingdom?

Prayer: *I am weary, Lord, of living in a land of lies. It seems that everyone is deluding themselves. But I thank you that at the end of the day I can trust myself to the light of your face. Amen.*

Psalm 5
Individual Lament

⁷ But I, by your great love,
    can come into your house;
in reverence I bow down
    toward your holy temple.

As I MAKE THESE first steps into the world of the Psalms, not only am I shocked by the jarring language but also struck by how liturgical things seem. Psalm 4, for example, ends with a prayer for peace through the night hours; Psalm 5 begins with a morning prayer of supplication. It's like we are tracking some kind of daily office. To pray these psalms is to say goodbye to the ridiculous notion of a 24/7 world and enter into a primordial rhythm of vespers and lauds.

In this particular psalm one might be forgiven for thinking that our early morning riser is maybe just a little bit too pious. There is so much here about the wicked not being welcome that by the time he enters the sanctuary in the early morning light it feels like we are being lured into a rant rather than prayer. As we step through the portals of the house of God, however, the thing that grips us, and that persuades us we are welcome, is not our piety but God's mercy. Once we understand this, everything else in the psalm flows—prayers for protection, prayers for guidance, even prayers for justice—because now it is not my righteousness I am being led into but God's righteousness.

Prayer: *Dear Lord, every time I pray Psalm 4 and 5, I am reminded of that anthem by Edwin Hatch which so beautifully conflates the two, and becomes my prayer here: "Lead me Lord, lead me in your righteousness, make your way plain before my face. For it is you Lord, you Lord only, that maketh me dwell in safety."*

Psalm 6
Individual Lament

⁴ Turn, LORD, and deliver me;
   save me because of your unfailing love.
⁵ Among the dead no one proclaims your name.
   Who praises you from the grave?

YOU DON'T REALIZE HOW polite your prayers have become until you pray the Psalms. Our prayers are polite because we assume that politeness is what piety amounts to. And given that politeness requires deference, soon enough these prayers become incredibly passive. How bored the Almighty must be! There is nothing he loves more than a good tussle, but all he seems to get from his saints is obsequiousness.

How different things are in the Psalms. Here, there is not a pious platitude in sight. Already, these first five psalms have drawn from us a bluntness that would shock even a northerner. When the psalmist starts twisting God's arm to heal him, even I'm wondering whether we are on the borders of irreverence. The occasion permits it I suppose. There is nothing like being on the verge of death to elicit dirty tricks. And the thing is, it works. Just pray the psalm through. Because, sickness or no, the heart of prayer is not resignation but wrestling.

Prayer: *Forgive me, Lord, for offering you dull and oftentimes dishonest prayers. Give me the courage to pray like the psalmist, even if it means shocking myself out of my piety. Amen.*

Psalm 7
Individual Lament

¹⁴ Whoever is pregnant with evil
    conceives trouble and gives birth to disillusionment.
¹⁵ Whoever digs a hole and scoops it out
    falls into the pit they have made.

THERE CAN BE NO more wonderful feeling in the world than that of vindication. Knowing that God has noticed how badly we have been treated and, furthermore, has taken action to put the record straight has a delicious taste to it, especially when it ends up with our enemies falling into the very hole they had been digging for us. It makes us feel that there is justice in the world after all. The trouble is, life is not that simple. Sometimes it takes years for the truth to come out. Meantime, like David, we have to live with the anguish of watching lesser men triumph. Who is Cush anyway? He ought to be a footnote, not a victor.

Psalm 7 reminds us, however, that it is comfort enough sometimes to simply lodge our case with God: to state the righteousness of our cause; to enjoin the lion who is God to rise; and to conjure up images in our mind of how the wicked will come to a terrible end. We may even find ourselves thanking God for his victory, even though no victory is in sight. But what we will be thanking him for in the end is not our righteousness but his.

Prayer: *Lord, I am well aware I can deceive myself, so maybe I really am to blame. But where I am not, please affirm me in the justice of my cause. Amen.*

Psalm 8
Creation

³ When I consider your heavens,
    the work of your fingers,
the moon and the stars,
    which you have set in place,
⁴ what is mankind that you are mindful of them,
    human beings that you care for them?

AFTER FIVE CONSECUTIVE PSALMS brim full of suffering, what a contrast to arrive at the gates of Psalm 8. It's as if we've returned to Eden. And coming to prayer feeling jaded, as we so often do, by the language of the market, it is a welcome relief to find ourselves back again in a world of wonder. The vastness of everything, the sheer scale of the universe, is not a pretext for unbelief—not a reason for thinking we are lost in the cosmos—but a prelude for worship. We marvel with the psalmist at the mindfulness of God. It turns out we are special after all. Indeed, as we look up into the starry night, happy to be alive in such an enchanted garden, what astonishes us is not just its majesty but its delicacy, because what we discern there is not simply the work of his hands but the skill of his fingers. I call to mind the words of Annie Dillard: "we are a faint tracing on the surface of a mystery."

Prayer: *Dear Lord, I cannot help thinking, as I pray this psalm, of the children who made such a glorious din as Jesus entered the city of Jerusalem (Matt 21:16); and I join with them in believing that his crushed divinity is indeed the glory of man. Amen.*

Psalm 9
Individual Lament

¹⁶ The LORD is known by his acts of justice;
the wicked are ensnared by the work of their hands.
¹⁷ The wicked go down to the realm of the dead,
all the nations that forget God.
¹⁸ But God will never forget the needy;
the hope of the afflicted will never perish.

ARROGANCE HAS A CERTAIN swagger. It believes itself to be above the law. What the arrogant forget, however, is that God is on the side of the oppressed. In fact, he is as passionate about justice as he is about anything. It may seem by the look of some of those scripture posters that God loves nothing more than a few lambs gambolling on a hillside, but in truth he is a terror: relentless in his pursuit of righteousness and peace. If we have a problem with that, if it offends our sensibilities, we had better stop praying these Psalms right now, for wherever one looks in the Psalms one is overcome by this theme. The very next psalm flows out of this slightly shorter psalm, thus providing a double warning for anyone who thinks the Lord has turned a blind eye. And it's not that God is a Marxist; nor that the Bible promotes the liberal view of progress; rather, that prayer really does serve notice on the powerful in the land, alerting them to the fact that God is capable of great reversals. The wicked fall into the pit they have set for others, whilst those who face the gates of death find themselves standing at the gates of Jerusalem. No wonder the psalmist gives thanks.

Prayer: *Dear Lord, I am surprised that you are so passionate about justice. I thought you were only concerned with things like worship and prayer. Please fill me with this same passion, so that I can take my place in the affairs of the world. Amen.*

Psalm 10

Individual Lament

¹⁶ The LORD is King for ever and ever;
    the nations will perish from his land.
¹⁷ You, LORD, hear the desire of the afflicted;
    you encourage them, and you listen to their cry,
¹⁸ defending the fatherless and the oppressed,
    so that mere earthly mortals
    will never again strike terror.

Mᴇᴍᴏʀɪᴄɪᴅᴇ ɪs ᴀ ᴡᴏʀᴅ I came across recently: the idea that even the memory of a people can be eradicated from history. It is often used in the context of colonial aggression—the bulldozing of names and places. In Psalm 9 we could use the word to describe the actions of God, who in his great reversal of things commits memoricide against those who persecute the poor. And it reminds us, if we haven't realized it already, that praying these psalms is not for the faint hearted. We come to the Psalms expecting to find sweet devotionals; instead we uncover swift retributions.

Here in Psalm 10 (which in all probability started out its life as the second half of Psalm 9), the assault on tyranny continues, this time in the form of lament and supplication: lament over the unaccountability of the wicked; supplication for the vindication of the lowly. And the reason it is important that we own these two psalms, not skipping a single letter of the acrostic which binds them together, is because without this solidarity with the poor our faith will always be suspect—nothing more than suburban piety.

Prayer: *O God, thank you for challenging me early on in this journey into the Psalms that the work of prayer only just begins when I get up off my knees. Help me to see that true religion is looking after the widow and the orphan. Amen.*

Psalm 11

Individual Lament

⁴ The Lᴏʀᴅ is in his holy temple;
   the Lᴏʀᴅ is on his heavenly throne.
He observes everyone on earth;
   his eyes examine them.
⁵ The Lᴏʀᴅ examines the righteous,
   but the wicked, those who love violence,
   he hates with a passion.

Tʜᴇʀᴇ ᴀʀᴇ ᴘʟᴀᴄᴇs ɪɴ the world where violence against the community of faith is a real and present threat. What on earth should you do? As far as the friends of the psalmist are concerned, the answer is obvious: flee like a bird. If you stick around you are likely to lose your life. But however tempting this might be, fleeing would represent a massive denial of faith, because for all the threats of the terrorists there is something more gripping than the terror of men and that is the face of God. The psalmist knows this, of course. In fact, he wonders why his friends don't know this. Mountains have their appeal to be sure, but there is no safer place than the sanctuary of God. In the face to face encounter of worship, the imminence of violence is overtaken by the immediacy of God's presence. There is even a sense in which sanctuary for the righteous triggers judgment for the wicked. In other words, while we worship the world gets sorted. But be that as it may, our preoccupation now is not with the destruction of the Sodom and Gomorrahs of our world but with the blessing of Aaron.

Prayer: *The Lord bless you and keep you. The Lord make his face shine upon you and be gracious to you. The Lord turn his face toward you, and give you his peace. Amen.*

Psalm 12

Community Lament

³ May the LORD silence all flattering lips
   and every boastful tongue—
⁴ those who say,
   "By our tongues we will prevail;
   our own lips will defend us—who is lord over us?"

IT TAKES A PROPHET to say things as they really are. And it takes a prophetic psalm, which this one is, to pray it: to pray the deep grief so many feel about living in a world where good old fashioned things like truth, fidelity, and love are treated with derision, while honor is given to things that in any other age would be regarded as vice, such as deceit, boasting, and lust. Perhaps the worst of it, as far as any prophet is concerned, is that it is all glossed over with smooth talk. In the world of Vanity Fair the art of flattery is one of the first things you learn. But the truth is we are dealing with "barbarians in pin stripe suits." Behind all the spin lies an evil intent.

In praying all this, one has to be careful of ranting of course. On the other hand, why else is this psalm here but to give us an opportunity from time to time to express our anger to God at the sheer arrogance of those in the public square, as well as our heart-felt desire that he might bring them to account.

Prayer: *Make us people of substance, Lord. Deliver us from this slimy charm that we live in, and give us words that have been proven by fire. Amen.*

Psalm 13
Individual Lament

¹ How long, LORD? Will you forget me forever?
   How long will you hide your face from me?
² How long must I wrestle with my thoughts
   and day after day have sorrow in my heart?
   How long will my enemy triumph over me?

AS A RECOVERING MELANCHOLIC, I'm not sure how good this psalm is for me. I am trying to get free from self-pity, not indulge in it. Yet, when the cycle of prayer brings me once again to this short plaintive poem—perhaps the purest lament you will ever find—I am greatly relieved. Yes, it's a bit exaggerated. To question whether the Lord has forgotten me forever does sound a touch melodramatic. But what it creates nonetheless is permission to see our sadness not as an aberration from the norm—the medicalization of sadness—but as a legitimate response to things that happen. Sometimes the sadness is so overwhelming that it really does feel as if the Lord has forgotten us.

Paradoxically, by giving voice to this question, we actually place ourselves on the road to recovery. For it is only when we are bold to pray "How long?" that hope begins to rise. Just ask those who heard Martin Luther King Jr. By giving voice to the unmentionable, we lay hold of the unimaginable: that all suffering has an end, and that one day, maybe sooner than we think, we will live in the joy of requited love.

Prayer: *Thank you, gracious Father, that you allow me to ask you the most searching questions, and then answer me with unfailing love and unspeakable joy. Amen.*

Psalm 14

Community Lament

[4] Do all these evildoers know nothing?
   They devour my people as though eating bread;
      they never call on the LORD.
[5] But there they are, overwhelmed with dread,
      for God is present in the company of the righteous.
[6] You evildoers frustrate the plans of the poor,
      but the LORD is their refuge.

IT WAS THE RUSSIAN writer Solzhenitsyn who said, in seeking to explain the sorry history of his own country: "Men have forgotten God. That is why all this has happened." At the time, people were shocked. But it is nothing that the psalmist hasn't already noted by way of a diagnostic on the moral turpitude of the nation. And while these prayers are a bit extreme, with nothing good to say about anyone, maybe sometimes it is just good to pray this stuff off our chest: to express our dismay over the widespread corruption of culture, but also to affirm our belief that the decline into decadence is so often the forerunner of cultural renaissance. St. Paul believed this. The bewilderment of the psalmist in finding not one righteous person becomes for the apostle the prelude to the good news of Jesus (Rom 3:11–12). Subsequent history has followed that gospel instinct. When the night is at its darkest, a new dawn is just around the corner, for God is present in the company of the righteousness. So yes, the fool may say in his heart "there is no God," and act accordingly. But in the end it is not the market that prevails, nor communism for that matter, but the prayers of a few old saints.

Prayer: *I thank you God that despite all appearances your purposes will ultimately prevail. Keep me from despair and let your joy be my strength. Amen.*

Psalm 15
Entrance Liturgy

¹ LORD, who may dwell in your sacred tent?
  Who may live on your holy mountain?
² The one whose walk is blameless,
  who does what is righteous,
  who speaks the truth from their heart;

IN PRAYING THE PSALMS *seriatim*—that is, in sequence—every once in a while you get a reminder that for all their personal appeal these prayers are never too far away from the precincts of worship. This psalm brings us right up to the entrance of the temple, warning us that it is a risky thing to pass through its gates. The demands that are placed upon us are exacting to say the least—a decalogue full in fact.

Given this is so, we might shrink back from praying this psalm. It all feels a bit too heavy. But if we stay with the psalm long enough we discover that this is not the case. As the priest asks who is fit to dwell in the presence of God, what we then recount in our praying are not the demands of morality, as such, but the beauty of holiness: a vision of life in all its entirety, in word, thought, and deed. There is nothing here we don't know of course. We find echoes of all the psalms we have prayed thus far: much is made of the way we speak; justice once again features as the heart of God; we are reminded that holiness is always costly. Above all, we celebrate that for all the short-term gain of shady living the righteous shall never be shaken.

Prayer: *Forgive me, Lord, if I have ever approached you casually. You deserve better. And not only in the sanctuary but in the everydayness of my life. Amen.*

Psalm 16

Individual Lament

⁵ LORD, you alone are my portion and my cup;
　　you make my lot secure.
⁶ The boundary lines have fallen for me in pleasant places;
　　surely I have a delightful inheritance.
⁷ I will praise the LORD, who counsels me;
　　even at night my heart instructs me.
⁸ I keep my eyes always on the LORD.
　　With him at my right hand, I will not be shaken.

HAVING PRAYED A TENTH of the Psalter already, a number of images have started to repeat, none more so than the image of God as a refuge for those who trust in him. It is a delightful vision, if not a cosy one. In praying it we are welcomed into the hospitality of God's sanctuary, which is where we truly belong, while God, in a now familiar triangle, takes care of our enemies. Indeed, the joy expressed about being under the roof of God, free at last from idols, is so intense that we sense we are praying the words of a recent convert in the first flush of enthusiasm. Everything is here: resolve to truly repent; realization that God alone can satisfy; contentment with how good things are; and a simple commitment to trust at all times, in the confidence that with the Lord at my side I will never be shaken. It's good to pray like this again. It feels fresh and innocent. It's like a second naivety. In this frame of mind one could believe in anything—even resurrection (Acts 2:25–28).

Prayer: *Lord, why would I look to anyone else but you? The boundary lines truly have fallen for me in pleasant places. You have the words of eternal life. Amen.*

Psalm 17

Individual Lament

⁷ Show me the wonders of your great love,
  you who save by your right hand
  those who take refuge in you from their foes.
⁸ Keep me as the apple of your eye;
  hide me in the shadow of your wings
⁹ from the wicked who are out to destroy me,
  from my mortal enemies who surround me.

LIFE IS TOUGH. WHOEVER said it wouldn't be? Fortunately, we have a song book in the Bible that accurately reflects this. In fact, it seems that these early psalms have been about little else but trouble and strife, with one or two reprieves in between. When things get like that, we want more than anything for God to rise up to destroy our foes. We may even venture into the forbidden world of vengeance. Both are prayed in this psalm. But more deeply felt than both of these instincts, and ultimately more powerful, is the simple awareness that no matter how bad things become we are the apple of God's eye. Actually, that is all we need to know. When life gets hard, and we feel we can't go on, it's enough to sense that God is just sitting there gazing at us.

To pray this psalm, then, is to anticipate a lull in the storm. In the midst of violence, it is to feel the protection of God's mothering wing. And finally, having spent far too much time in a world of over-sated, dew-lapped faces, it is to wake up one morning and find oneself beside the face of God.

Prayer: *Dear Lord, I know I cannot escape from the world. But it is good to know that I can stay in the shadow of your wings. Amen.*

Psalm 18
Royal

¹⁶ He reached down from on high and took hold of me;
    he drew me out of deep waters.
¹⁷ He rescued me from my powerful enemy,
    from my foes, who were too strong for me.
¹⁸ They confronted me in the day of my disaster,
    but the LORD was my support.
¹⁹ He brought me out into a spacious place;
    he rescued me because he delighted in me.

THERE IS NOTHING SANGUINE about a life of faith. It appears that crisis is a prerequisite. Eden, Sinai, and Calvary are all testimony to the perverse theology that God only seems to act when we are in a hole. The flip side of this liking for a tragedy is that victory, when it comes, as here in Psalm 18, is all the more dramatic: thunderous theophanies; eleventh hour rescues; one minute in the clutches of death, next minute standing on the heights. Why, it sings like a good Welsh hymn!

If, for you, faith is about being nice and kind then you won't get this psalm because it works on the level of what P. T. Forsyth describes as "the soul's despair and breathless gratitude." It gives expression to what Tolkien coined as a *eucatastrophe*: a sudden and very great reversal, giving rise to ecstatic thanks and praise. That it takes up fifty verses means that you need to take a deep breath before you pray it. But even though you will be stretched out by the end, it will be worth it. This is David at his best, and the gospel in the raw.

Prayer: *Lord, I thank you that despite all the toils and snares of my life you continue to bring me into a spacious place. Amen.*

Psalm 19
Creation

¹ The heavens declare the glory of God;
   the skies proclaim the work of his hands.
² Day after day they pour forth speech;
   night after night they reveal knowledge.
³ They have no speech, they use no words;
   no sound is heard from them.
⁴ Yet their voice goes out into all the earth,
   their words to the ends of the world.

THERE IS NO MORE powerful speech than silence. The "unheard sounds" of God's creation are so resonant that they reach to the ends of the earth. No less effective than the silent preaching of God's glory, however, is the radiance of God's sun. Running his race from one end of the earth to the other, there is no one who cannot feel the warmth of his rays. No wonder some are tempted to worship this bridegroom. Of all the idolatries it seems the most likely.

Yet, for all the splendor of God's pavilioned world, no one gets saved by a sunset. As the psalmist rightly adduces, we need the light of God's word. For it is here, in the scrolls of scripture, that we are fully addressed as human beings made in the image of God. And it's not that the word is any less sensual than a sunset. Not at all. Eating the word of God oftentimes leaves us with honey dripping from our mouths. But for all the sensuality, it is serious nonetheless, for by these words we are sustained as well as exposed.

It seems apt that the last verse, which offers heartfelt meditation, is recited in silent prayer three times daily in Jewish worship. It's as if the silence of God's creation finds its way into silence of our hearts.

Prayer: *O Lord my Redeemer, I join with the silent prayers of your ancient people by saying three times daily, "may the words of my mouth and this meditation of my heart be pleasing in your sight." Amen.*

Psalm 20
Royal

⁶ Now this I know:
  The LORD gives victory to his anointed.
He answers him from his heavenly sanctuary
  with the victorious power of his right hand.
⁷ Some trust in chariots and some in horses,
  but we trust in the name of the LORD our God.

HORSES AND CHARIOTS WERE symbols of military power—a source of national pride. The more an army has, the more it can assert itself in the world. Not so with you, however—recalling the words of the future anointed (Mark 10:43). To be God's exceptional people is, by definition, to renounce such crude posturing, not to mention national jingoism, and simply wait for the Lord to arise. And it's not that he is unwilling to act. On the contrary, as you pray this royal psalm you'll sound every bit the prosperity preacher as you prophecy abundant blessings "in the name of the Lord." The language of victory is our native tongue, after all. But it is not a shrill victory, nor presumptuous faith. Rather, it is a quiet and settled confidence that as we watch and pray something is being done in the world, as Niebuhr points out, that is divine "both in its threat and in its promise." Every time I recite the words of this psalm I am reminded that prayer is a kind of active waiting. It's what makes prayer so painfully dispossessing and yet so utterly engaging.

Prayer: *Lord, it is so tempting to take the world on with the world's weapons. Teach me instead to simply trust in your goodness. Amen.*

Psalm 21
Royal

⁵ Through the victories you gave, his glory is great;
  you have bestowed on him splendor and majesty.
⁶ Surely you have granted him unending blessings
  and made him glad with the joy of your presence.
⁷ For the king trusts in the LORD;
  through the unfailing love of the Most High
  he will not be shaken.

MY HEBREW PROFESSOR AT seminary was a very devout man. With his long grey beard and piercing eyes, I imagined him to be a prophet. At the beginning of every class he would pray pretty much the same thing, which was that God would renew our strength for the task ahead (not a bad prayer when one thinks of the challenge of learning Hebrew). My guess is that he was borrowing from this royal psalm, for its header and footer is the strength of the Lord. Indeed there is nothing that happens in this psalm without the strength of the Lord. It may, on the surface, appear to celebrate our victories, but in truth everything is gift. Without those series of "You's" in the first half of the psalm, nothing is going to happen. And even when we get to the king in the second half of the poem, and start to revel in his conquests, we are left in no doubt as to who is behind it all.

One suspects that this is a prayer that Hezekiah would be very comfortable with, or someone like Josiah—or David of course. Supremely among the kings they relied not on their own strength but on God's unfailing love. The challenge will be for us to live likewise: to not press ahead as some self-styled hero, battling against the odds, but to conceive all of life as weakness bracketed by strength (2 Cor 12:10).

Prayer: *As I begin this day, tempted to struggle on in my own strength, teach me once again to rely upon you. Amen.*

Psalm 22
Individual Lament

¹ My God, my God, why have you forsaken me?
    Why are you so far from saving me,
      so far from my cries of anguish?
  ² My God, I cry out by day, but you do not answer,
      by night, but I find no rest.

IT IS ALMOST IMPOSSIBLE to pray this psalm without hearing it as Jesus' last words on the cross: "My God my God, why have you forsaken me?" When I get to this psalm, I am tempted to take my shoes and socks off. This is holy ground. Yet, as much as I approach Psalm 22 as a station of the cross, I also embrace it as a personal lament, for this is *my* loneliness that is being described here, *my* forsakenness, *my* feelings of abandonment. For sure, I cannot even begin to imagine the desolation that Jesus felt on the cross, but I can identify with the sheer terror the psalmist feels as the darkness closes in. It is a kind of crucifixion, affecting every part of my body, and leaving me with a profound sense of the absence of God.

The appearance of Psalm 22 in the Psalter assures us that there is no shame in throwing our questions at God. Abandonment is not a feeling to be tidied away but something to be prayed. Our questioning of God is a sign of deep faith. Who else could experience the acuteness of absence other than a person familiar with presence? Who else but an intimate with God could remind him of his covenant duties? As we pray the psalm, it becomes clear that the "my" in the opening line is not simply a possessive pronoun but a mark of possessive love.

Prayer: *I am grateful, Lord, as I pray this psalm, that there is light in the depth of my darkness. But I am also grateful for the space to ask my questions and to know your strength. Amen.*

Psalm 23

Trust Psalm

^{4} Even though I walk
    through the darkest valley,
I will fear no evil,
    for you are with me;
your rod and your staff,
    they comfort me.

BEFORE YOU PRAY THIS psalm, put aside, if you can, images of lush, rolling countryside with picture-postcard sheep wandering lazily down to a quiet lake. Instead, think barren wilderness; scorching heat; sudden blinding storms; water shortages; loose rocks; bandits at large; a shepherd desperate to find his lost sheep and bring it home. Once you have done that, maybe then you will be getting nearer to the heart of this much loved but overworked psalm. For this is no quaint pastoral, but more like a spiritual odyssey in which, at some point, we will have to pass through one of those narrow ravines in order to get to our destination. There is literally no escape. Much as you would love to go round it, you have to go through it. However, even though the silence is eerie, and even though we feel exposed, strangely, says the psalmist, "I fear no evil," for the truth is we are not alone. There, in the dark defile of my life, with cudgel in one hand and crook in the other, my Pastor walks ahead of me, relentless in his commitment to get me to the other side. And what awaits me there is a banquet, for it turns out that what has been pursuing me all this time are not the wolves of my imagination but the goodness of the Lord.

Prayer: *Wouldn't it be wonderful, Lord, if I could live less anxiously, content to rest in your shade? So my prayer today is for your perfect love to cast out fear. Amen.*

Psalm 24
Entrance Liturgy

¹ The earth is the Lord's, and everything in it,
   the world, and all who live in it;
² for he founded it on the seas
   and established it on the waters.
³ Who may ascend the mountain of the Lord?
   Who may stand in his holy place?
⁴ The one who has clean hands and a pure heart,
   who does not trust in an idol
   or swear by a false god.

THERE SHOULD ALWAYS BE a touch of glory about the worship of God. The moment we sense an over familiarity creeping in, or a mincing pietism, we ought to resist. Psalm 24 helps us do that. To pray it is to enter into big country; it is to fill our lungs with an anthem of majesty; it is to believe that there is nothing and nowhere in this wonderful world of ours that is outside of the purview of God. The earth is the Lord's and the fullness thereof.

Such a universal faith, such a catholic vision, calls for an uncompromising faith of course. No place here for idols. But more than personal holiness is reverential awesomeness: holy places gathering the faithful; antiphonal choirs roused in expectation; ancient doors thrown off their hinges, so that the King of Glory might come in. Anything less is not worship but entertainment.

Prayer: *O God, how we long for glory in the church. Deliver us from bland religiosity and let us experience the weight of glory that comes from knowing you. Amen.*

Psalm 25

Individual Lament

⁴ Show me your ways, LORD,
   teach me your paths.
⁵ Guide me in your truth and teach me,
   for you are God my Savior,
   and my hope is in you all day long.
⁶ Remember, LORD, your great mercy and love,
   for they are from of old.
⁷ Do not remember the sins of my youth
   and my rebellious ways;
according to your love remember me,
   for you, LORD, are good.

I SUSPECT MANY OF us have a very negative view of God. Where it comes from is an interesting question, but it has left many of us with an image of someone who is just waiting for us to step out of line. In this psalm, however, we learn that God is surprisingly lenient about our humanity—our wayward youth in particular. We learn that the very core of his nature is mercy and steadfast love. He remembers not our sins but his love. Where we are faithless, he is faithful. If we are to fear anything it is not falling into the hands of God but the hands of men, for there, so often, we will find no mercy at all. What he does require of us, however, is wholeheartedness: the willingness to daily lift up our souls to him; to bring the whole of our life before the whole of him; and to wait on him even when we don't understand what is going on. If we live like this, asking God to guide us in his ways, we will be living in the fear of the Lord, which is not a synonym for dread but an epithet for awe.

Prayer: *Lord, help me to trust that you are so much more gracious than I could possibly imagine, and so much more demanding than I should settle for. Amen.*

Psalm 26

Individual Lament

⁴ I do not sit with the deceitful,
   nor do I associate with hypocrites.
⁵ I abhor the assembly of evildoers
   and refuse to sit with the wicked.
⁶ I wash my hands in innocence,
   and go about your altar, LORD,
⁷ proclaiming aloud your praise
   and telling of all your wonderful deeds.

ANYONE WHO KNOWS JESUS' Parable of the Pharisee and the Tax Collector in Luke's Gospel will wonder if we have here a psalm of similar self-righteousness. All the same elements appear to be present, including the spatial distance between the sanctimonious and the sinners. You could pretty much overlay the psalm into the parable and see the prayer as an expansion of the line: "I thank you, Lord, that I am not like other people"—except, however, for two small but crucial differences. First, that this is no claim for sinlessness but a plea of innocence—a desire for vindication against a false charge. And second, that no matter how innocent the petitioner claims to be, what he ends up celebrating in the sanctuary is not his piety but God's unfailing love. For in the end everything is gift—even our integrity. The fact that any of us find ourselves in the congregation of God's people, in the house where he dwells, is a sheer wonder.

Prayer: *Lord, as I go about your altar, declaring aloud your praise, keep me from the way of wickedness but also from the sin of self-righteousness. Amen.*

Psalm 27

Individual Lament

⁴ One thing I ask from the LORD,
   this only do I seek:
that I may dwell in the house of the LORD
   all the days of my life,
to gaze on the beauty of the LORD
   and to seek him in his temple.
⁵ For in the day of trouble
   he will keep me safe in his dwelling;
he will hide me in the shelter of his sacred tent
   and set me high upon a rock.

PSALM 27 IS A particular favorite of many believers. Simply to pray it is a kind of therapy in which we speak faith to ourselves, over against the fears that could so easily cripple us. From beginning to end, we assert our trust in God to rescue us from our foes, both real and imagined. After all, here is a God who cannot forsake me. Even if everyone else forsakes me, God cannot, such is the loyalty of his love. In v. 4, however, the psalm takes a strange turn—something of a *non sequitur* it seems. Having begun in a strident fashion, it seems we have retreated, rather abruptly, from warfare to worship—so much so that some scholars think a different psalm has been inserted here. Indeed, I might have thought that myself, except that I belong to a worshipping community, in which case the discrepancy is easily resolved, for what better antidote to fear could there be but the abditory—the hiding place—of God's sanctuary. And it's not that we can hide away forever. At some point we have to face our enemies. But by spending time in the deep recesses of his shelter, gazing into the face of God, it's as if we grow stronger, more assured even, in the triumph of goodness.

Prayer: *Dear Lord, I truly believe that the world will be saved by beauty— your beauty. Give me courage to believe this and to do the one thing needful, which is to sit at your feet. Amen.*

Psalm 28

Individual Lament

¹ To you, LORD, I call;
  you are my Rock,
  do not turn a deaf ear to me.
For if you remain silent,
  I will be like those who go down to the pit.
² Hear my cry for mercy
  as I call to you for help,
as I lift up my hands
  toward your Most Holy Place.

I HAVE A BOOK on my shelf entitled *Prayers Plainly Spoken*. It is a collection of prayers written by Stanley Hauerwas for use in the chapel at Duke University, where he was a professor. The students insisted he publish them as they were keen for the honesty of his praying to reach a wider audience. The antecedents of his plain speaking, disarming prayers are the Psalms of course, and none more so than Psalm 28. Talk about direct! When was the last time you told God not to turn a deaf ear? Or try to manipulate him into action by clever logic? The boldness borders on impertinent. Yet, it seems to work. Somehow the combination of wit and humor appeals to the Lord, and he answers with stunning effect. Hence, what begins as a psalm of supplication ends as a psalm of praise. What starts with the specter of Sheol, the grave, finishes with us high upon a Rock. All because of prayer. And it's not that God is persuaded by our wit; nor that he is desperate for our praise. The loss of our particular voice will barely register in the festive throng of God's people. And yet it will register. For this is no despot we have come to worship but a shepherd who tends his flock and sometimes bears his lambs in his arms.

Prayer: *Lord, just when I think that my prayers are a dialogue of the deaf, you surprise me with stunning answers. I praise you, my Shepherd King. Amen.*

Psalm 29
General Hymn

⁷ The voice of the LORD strikes
   with flashes of lightning.
⁸ The voice of the LORD shakes the desert;
   the LORD shakes the Desert of Kadesh.
⁹ The voice of the LORD twists the oaks
   and strips the forests bare.
And in his temple all cry, "Glory!"

AS I PRAY THIS psalm I cannot help think of the Cornish evangelist Billy Bray. Asked once why it was he sang and shouted so much, why it was that he was a bit over the top, he replied: "if they were to put me in a barrel, I would shout *glory* out through the bunghole." That we might consider this extreme says as much about us as it does about Bray's eccentricity. It betrays the fact that most of us have grown up in a highly controlled environment with little or no room for wonder; whereas the real world—the strange world of the Psalms—is "charged with the grandeur of God" (Hopkins). Sweeping down over the northern forests of the Lebanon, down across the central mountains to the hot southern deserts of Kadesh, there is no place where his voice is not heard. His thunderous word leaves nothing unturned. Great cedars lie twisted; mighty oaks are broken; even the watery chaos submits to his bidding—such is the power of his majesty.

Prayer: *O God, we can put up with lots of things but what we cannot put up with is "itsy bitsy" religion. Give us glory, Lord, stark and uncontrolled. Amen.*

Psalm 30
Individual Psalm of Thanksgiving

⁴ Sing the praises of the LORD, you his faithful people;
   praise his holy name.
⁵ For his anger lasts only a moment,
   but his favor lasts a lifetime;
weeping may stay for the night,
   but rejoicing comes in the morning.

THERE'S NOTHING LIKE AN experience of being rescued from the brink to elicit thanks and praise. Gratitude, as Barth pointed out, is the reflex of grace—amazing grace even. In fact, you begin to wonder, in praying a psalm like this, whether faith can ever really emerge until you've known the pits. As anyone who has been baptized will tell you: it's not until you've grieved your sins, been stripped bare to your mortality, and then been clothed in the garments of the gospel that your feet begin to dance. Hence, as much as this is a dark psalm—full of that black humor we have seen before—it is also a joyful psalm. It is joyful at the point at which it is despairing (just as it is honest at the point at which the psalmist is most fragile), for the good news is that anger in God is only momentary—as momentary as a bad night that is dispelled by the mercy of a new morning. And having passed through it, having journeyed through the dark night of the soul, we discover that life is not diminished but enriched, for joy is not really joy until it has first wept.

Prayer: *Lord, I thank you that my raggedness does not disqualify me from faith but seems to be essential to the experience of your grace. Even so, let joy come in the morning. Amen.*

Psalm 31
Individual Lament

³ Since you are my rock and my fortress,
   for the sake of your name lead and guide me.
⁴ Keep me free from the trap that is set for me,
   for you are my refuge.
⁵ Into your hands I commit my spirit;
   deliver me, LORD, my faithful God.

IT IS A STRANGE fact of spiritual and religious life that those who speak for God so often become the victims of ridicule and scorn. Just ask Jeremiah. Or ask any regular preacher trying as best he or she can to be true to the word of God. After so many years of enduring this kind of treatment, you are left physically exhausted. And the hurt that comes with being maligned, or worse still simply ignored, can cut right to the bone. You feel like a pariah, not a prophet.

Where does one go with the sadness that accrues from all of this? Book I of the Psalter (1–41) is pretty much a relentless exhortation to take it to God. For it is only when we pray our complaint that we can possibly receive the comfort of God's refuge, as well as the knowledge that in the end the proud will be held to account for their lies.

These prayers may not be easy to pray. They require a candour that most of us are unpracticed in. But this is why the Psalms are here: to tutor us in honesty. Jesus prayed this prayer of course. Along with Psalm 22, this psalm contains one of the seven words from the cross. Caught in a maelstrom of hatred and slander concerning his own teaching, Jesus commits his spirit—the whole of his life—into his Father's hands.

Prayer: *Lord, I choose to believe that there is no period of history so godless, and no sadness so overwhelming, that we cannot trust that our times are in your hands. Amen.*

Psalm 32
Wisdom

³ When I kept silent,
   my bones wasted away
   through my groaning all day long.
⁴ For day and night
   your hand was heavy on me;
my strength was sapped
   as in the heat of summer.
⁵ Then I acknowledged my sin to you
   and did not cover up my iniquity.
I said, "I will confess
   my transgressions to the LORD."
And you forgave
   the guilt of my sin.

GUILT CAN ONLY BE held in for so long. To take a macabre image from an Edgar Allan Poe play, it's only a question of time before, finally, the dead bodies shout out from underneath the floorboards. The energy required to silence one's conscience is so sapping that not just psalmists but even secular psychologists are coming to see that good old-fashioned confession brings great relief. What better feeling in the world can there be, what greater blessing, than to confess and to know that you are forgiven? Which makes you wonder why we are so reluctant to come out in the open. After all, no one is expecting perfection. Not even the Lord. He is well aware our frailty. A basic definition of a saint is not someone who is perfect but someone who is humble—humble enough to know when one has done wrong. So my guess is that the concealment has a lot to do with pride, and a lot to do with the unreality of religion.

Prayer: *Lord, help me to be honest with you, and then lead me lovingly in the way I should go. Amen.*

Psalm 33
General Hymn

¹⁶ No king is saved by the size of his army;
   no warrior escapes by his great strength.
¹⁷ A horse is a vain hope for deliverance;
   despite all its great strength it cannot save.
¹⁸ But the eyes of the LORD are on those who fear him,
   on those whose hope is in his unfailing love,
¹⁹ to deliver them from death
   and keep them alive in famine.

FOR THOSE OF US raised in a culture where might is right, where aggression is celebrated as a virtue, it is difficult for us to believe that the heavens and the earth were created not by brute force but through speech—or as Robert Alter puts it in describing the theology behind this psalm: "not by a Big Bang but by measured words." But this is what is being praised here. Indeed, it is not only God's word that is praised but the wonderful as well as subversive truth that what lies at the heart of the universe is not violence but virtue—God's virtue of course, which is faithfulness, righteousness, and steadfast love.

Since this is the case, then the trick is to try to live in sync with this reality: to resist the myth of self-sufficiency and trust instead in the kindness of God. Such a stance will not be considered *realpolitik*. It will be mocked and scorned as naivety—as Sennacherib mocked Hezekiah in 2 Kings 18:19–26. But as the dawn breaks it will be the Assyrians, not the Israelites, who lie strewn on the ground—a testament to the proverbial wisdom that numbers are nothing compared to simple reliance on the Lord. No wonder the psalm begins as it does. Such a theme is worthy of a brand new composition, in the most public of settings, with the finest musicians.

Prayer: *Please, Lord, in a world obsessed by size and numbers, teach me simple reliance on the promise of your love. Amen.*

Psalm 34
Individual Psalm of Thanksgiving

[17] The righteous cry out, and the LORD hears them;
  he delivers them from all their troubles.
[18] The LORD is close to the brokenhearted
  and saves those who are crushed in spirit.

PREACHERS CAN OFTEN COME across as unreal, promising among other things to bring us into a land of pain-free existence. Not only is this an impossible dream, it is not even a proper reading of the texts. In Psalm 34 for instance, God does not promise to protect us from all harm—what is David doing in Gath in that case?—but rather to deliver us when we have been harmed. Likewise, God does not promise that our hearts will never be broken (I suspect that our hearts will be broken many times before we are done with this life), but that when we are brokenhearted he will be near us. Which means that this psalm is both a relief and a joy. A relief because who has not felt some time or other on the edge of madness? And a joy because no matter what the circumstances God can be trusted to pull us through. Indeed, such is the power of his deliverance that by the end of the psalm you will have prayed a lot of words like "all," "never," and "no more." These bold, total words are not naivety on the part of the psalmist, but the truth: that the Lord is good.

Prayer: *Every time I come to your table, Lord, I taste and see that you are good. As I come away from your table, help me to be good, to live in the fear of the Lord. Amen.*

Psalm 35
Individual Lament

⁴ May those who seek my life
    be disgraced and put to shame;
may those who plot my ruin
    be turned back in dismay.
⁵ May they be like chaff before the wind,
    with the angel of the LORD driving them away;
⁶ may their path be dark and slippery,
    with the angel of the LORD pursuing them.

WHAT ON EARTH DO we do with this psalm? It's one thing to pray for deliverance from our enemies; quite another to wish ill upon them. Surely, if we have any sense of decency we ought to skip from Psalm 34 to 36 and leave Psalm 35 for the theologians to debate over. Yet, as much as this is an awkward psalm to pray, it is a necessary one. We ought to be thankful it made the collection, as well as others like it. For what these imprecatory psalms purchase for us is the freedom to say exactly how we feel—as long as we say it to God. Actually, in praying this way we are doing what we are supposed to do when we commit our vengeance to God, which is *to commit our vengeance to God*: that is, to actually say it, and not just theologically think it. These prayers may not change anything, but better say it to God than say it to someone's face. In fact, these psalms actually represent the height of faith, not its absence. As much as they rail against God over the injustice in the world, they also express a solid conviction, precisely at the point of doubt, that he will have the final word. Such is the paradox of a questioning faith.

Prayer: *Lord, thank you that I can lodge my angriest thoughts to you in the knowledge that you will take care of things better than me. Amen.*

Psalm 36

Individual Lament

⁷ How priceless is your unfailing love, O God!
  People take refuge in the shadow of your wings.
⁸ They feast on the abundance of your house;
  you give them drink from your river of delights.
⁹ For with you is the fountain of life;
  in your light we see light.

THERE ARE SOME PEOPLE in this world who are so into themselves that it is simply impossible for them to self-critique. Rejecting any sense of transcendence—any notion of the Other who speaks over us—all these people do is flatter themselves into thinking that whatever they are thinking or doing at any one time is the only true morality. In the absence of a critical distance (or holy presence more like), transgression resides in their hearts. However, there are other people in the world who are the exact opposite. While the wicked plot mischief in the middle of the night, taking a stand on the way of no good, there are others who speak God's words when they lie down and when they get up and when they go on their way. For them, the world is not a self-referential bubble but "heaven in ordinary"—a sanctuary full of sensual delights. To use C. S. Lewis's image, life for the faithful gets bigger and bigger, as we drink our fill of the kindness of God; whereas "there" (v. 12), at a place far removed, things get smaller and smaller, as the arrogant come toppling down. For in the end, no matter how much the proud caress their egos, it is no match for a simple prayer of trust.

Prayer: *Lord, help me to stay open-hearted to you, satisfied with nothing less than your unfailing love. Amen.*

Psalm 37
Wisdom

⁷ Be still before the LORD
   and wait patiently for him;
do not fret when people succeed in their ways,
   when they carry out their wicked schemes.
⁸ Refrain from anger and turn from wrath;
   do not fret—it leads only to evil.
⁹ For those who are evil will be destroyed,
   but those who hope in the LORD will inherit the land.
¹⁰ A little while, and the wicked will be no more;
   though you look for them, they will not be found.
¹¹ But the meek will inherit the land
   and enjoy peace and prosperity.

IN SO FAR AS praying the Psalter is a kind of therapy (which is not as modern as it sounds), then the overall effect of this psalm is one of calm. And the way it fosters calm is to teach wisdom. In a world where success is the big thing, it counsels us to delight in God and trust him for the rest. At a time in our history where assertiveness has become a virtue, it reminds us of a beatitudinal truth that the meek will inherit the earth. When everyone around you seems to be on the make, looking after number one, it urges us to be generous "on every occasion." After all, who has ever seen the righteous go without? Actually, we all have. But even so, Psalm 37 encourages us to take a long view, to rehearse in our minds the world as it will be, so that when we do get up from prayer and enter the fray of the day somehow we won't be as distressed as we might have been. As the crowd goes on its noisy way, unconscious that it really is walking on thin ice, we will inhabit a holy quiet, for this psalm was forged at "the still turning point of the world."

Prayer: *Lord, I live in such a hurried, anxious world. Give me courage not to fret but to live quietly and humbly before you. Amen.*

Psalm 38

Individual Lament

¹ Lord, do not rebuke me in your anger
   or discipline me in your wrath.
² Your arrows have pierced me,
   and your hand has come down on me.
³ Because of your wrath there is no health in my body;
   there is no soundness in my bones because of my sin.
⁴ My guilt has overwhelmed me
   like a burden too heavy to bear.

SOME PSALMS ARE GOOD to read; others, like this penitential psalm, grate with us. And the reason they grate is because by and large we have lost the language of contrition. These days we talk about hang-ups or problems. As Eugene Peterson once quipped, we don't so much confess the sins of the fathers these days but the neuroses of the mothers. These penitential psalms are here, however, because there are some things in our lives that can only be dealt with by the old fashioned language of sin and guilt. And it's not that all suffering is a result of sin. There's enough even in this psalm to counter that pernicious doctrine. As the book of Job reminds us, there is such a thing as innocent suffering. But even so, if we are going to live healthy lives then once in a while we need words to put things right. And what is so heartening about this psalm is that the other side of penitence is a God who is wanting to forgive. In other words, if there is a connection between sin and suffering—and maybe, once in a while, there is—it is not broken by increased righteousness but by God's faithfulness. The last line of the psalm is the giveaway. It urges us to treat penitence not as a mechanism but a personal plea: "Come quickly to help me, my Lord and my Savior."

Prayer: *Merciful God, help me to own my sin in order that I can enjoy your mercy. Amen.*

Psalm 39
Individual Lament

⁴ "Show me, LORD, my life's end
    and the number of my days;
    let me know how fleeting my life is.
⁵ You have made my days a mere handbreadth;
    the span of my years is as nothing before you.
Everyone is but a breath,
    even those who seem secure.

THERE'S NOTHING LIKE A serious illness to cause one to reflect on the fragility of life—and its brevity of course. The realization that life might soon come to an end has a remarkable ability to change one's perspective. Whereas once the world seemed so secure, suddenly we are struck by how ephemeral everything is. In truth, says the psalmist, we are a mere breath, our lives just a shadow.

It's nothing that Job didn't discover in his own suffering; nor anything that the teacher in Ecclesiastes didn't warn his congregation about. Psalm 39 takes its place in a venerable tradition of philosophical reflection on the transience of life. What is different about Psalm 39, however, is that we are encouraged to pray our existential crisis. Unlike other psalms of supplication, our need for rescue has become not half as important as our need to ask ultimate questions: questions we all have about the meaning and the mystery of life. The fact we emerge from this psalm without many answers, and still subject to taunts, seems beside the point. It's enough simply to have broken our silence and voiced our angst before God. After all, not only can he hear our prayers but he can hear our tears as well. So even if we carry shame, and even if the sadness can sometimes be overwhelming, it can be more than met by the hope of his presence.

Prayer: *Lord, I am feeling very fragile right now. Nothing seems permanent, except your love. Thank you. Amen.*

Psalm 40
Individual Lament

⁶ Sacrifice and offering you did not desire—
  but my ears you have opened—
  burnt offerings and sin offerings you did not require.
⁷ Then I said, "Here I am, I have come—
  it is written about me in the scroll.
⁸ I desire to do your will, my God;
  your law is within my heart."

THIS PSALM SEEMS UPSIDE down. It starts with thanksgiving and ends in a prayer for rescue. In that respect it may well be an amalgam of two prayers. In the middle it takes a different turn again, sounding every bit as iconoclastic as one of the prophets. But what I love about this middle section, and why I relish praying these words, is that they take us beyond the mechanics of organized religion and into the realms of heart obedience. Here the big thing is not just sacrifice and offering but ears that have been dug open to hear the voice of God. The scroll that we bring to our worship is not the book of the Torah, which is irreplaceable of course, but a kind of personal memoir of how God has spoken in our lives. And our response overall is not simply the duty of obedience, which is one thing, but a burning desire to do God's will.

Does this mean we are down on organized religion? Not at all. We are a people of word and sacrament. But what this psalm invites us to do is go beyond the forms and into the heart of what they exist for. No wonder the writer to the Hebrews appropriated this psalm to Jesus (Heb 10:5–7), for Jesus is heart religion *par excellence*.

Prayer: *O Lord, take me deeper into you so that my obedience moves from duty to delight. Make me a lover as well as a servant. Amen.*

Psalm 41
Individual Psalm of Thanksgiving

⁷ All my enemies whisper together against me;
    they imagine the worst for me, saying,
⁸ "A vile disease has afflicted him;
    he will never get up from the place where he lies."
⁹ Even my close friend,
    someone I trusted,
one who shared my bread,
    has turned against me.
¹⁰ But may you have mercy on me, LORD;
    raise me up, that I may repay them.

AS WE COME TO the end of the first of the five books into which the Psalms have been edited (modelled on the Pentateuch), we rehearse the all-too-familiar situation of illness, alienation, and slander. Once again, as with a number of psalms we have already prayed, it has a Job-like feel about it, as well as echoes of the Jesus story. Who is Judas but the archetypal betrayer: someone we once shared bread with around the table but who now devastates us by his deviousness (John 13:18). What is fascinating, however, and possibly new to the Psalms, is the basis upon which our lamenter thinks God will raise him up from his sickbed: namely, his generosity to the poor. I suspect this is not sound theology, any more than it is sound theology to suggest that God's vindication of him can only be discerned by raising him up. But then prayer doesn't have to be theologically sound. In prayer we can say what we want, not what we ought to say. And let's face it, wouldn't it be wonderful if sometimes, every once in a while, God silenced our critics by doing something spectacular in our lives? I know it sounds a bit like sweet revenge but there's not one of us who couldn't say "Amen to that!"

Prayer: *It's one thing for an enemy to lift his heel against me. I could cope with that. But not a friend. Lord, somewhere in all of this have mercy on me and vindicate my cause. Amen.*

Book II

Psalm 42
Individual Lament

[5] Why, my soul, are you downcast?
   Why so disturbed within me?
Put your hope in God,
   for I will yet praise him,
   my Savior and my God.

THE PSALTER IS THE prayer book of the church: prayer, of course, being human speech addressed to God. What is less acknowledged, however, but no less spiritual in content, is that prayer is also speaking to our self: our self addressing our soul, if that doesn't sound too strange, in a kind of inner questioning. And it is important we do so. Too often we allow our soul to speak to our self—unchallenged as it were—convincing us how hopeless things are, whereas what we should do, as the psalmist does, is speak to our soul, reminding it that no matter how bleak things seem, and how full of sorrow our heart is, we have a God who can yet redeem. Three times, in fact, the psalmist asks why it is his soul is so bent over, and three times he urges his soul to put its hope in God. These refrains put shape to the psalm as a whole and guide the soul through parched deserts and stormy seas into the presence of God. Furthermore, as much as they are expressions of deep soul searching, these refrains are also testament to the power of liturgy, for it is only as we repeat the words that hope has any chance of emerging. Otherwise, what's the point of a psalm? Psalms are raw intensity condensed into rhythmical forms. They are exactly what a prayer book should be about.

Prayer: *O God, without in any way denying what I am feeling right now, I am going to speak faith to my soul, for I know that you are able to save me. Amen.*

Psalm 43

Individual Lament

³ Send me your light and your faithful care,
   let them lead me;
let them bring me to your holy mountain,
   to the place where you dwell.
⁴ Then I will go to the altar of God,
   to God, my joy and my delight.
I will praise you with the lyre,
   O God, my God.

PSALM 43 WAS ORIGINALLY part of Psalm 42, broken up for reasons that are not entirely clear to us. Maybe it has something to do with the fact that what started out as a lament has turned into a petition for God to deliver the psalmist from his enemies. It's not that the enemies have caused his distress, but they have made it worse by suggesting that God must have abandoned him. Despite their taunts, the psalmist is confident, however, that God will vindicate him and lead him out of the gloom of exile up to the mountain of his presence. In terms of the liturgy, it is as black and white as that. Nevertheless, if Psalm 42 is about the power of liturgy to get us out of a hole, Psalm 43 reminds us once again that the epitome of spiritual experience, the thing that lies at the end of our liturgical journey, is not a private hermitage in the woods but a gathered community in worship. It is the loss of this joyful throng that he laments in Psalm 42, and gladly what he anticipates here in Psalm 43. Indeed, one suspects it will be all the more joyful precisely because he despaired that he might never experience it again. What better instrument to celebrate such a drama than the harp. Alone among the instruments it can render both sadness and delight.

Prayer: *O God, there is no better place for me to be than in your presence and among your people. Thank you that through all the ups and downs of my life you keep bringing me back to this place. Amen.*

Psalm 44

Community Lament

¹⁷ All this came upon us,
   though we had not forgotten you;
   we had not been false to your covenant.
¹⁸ Our hearts had not turned back;
   our feet had not strayed from your path.
¹⁹ But you crushed us and made us a haunt for jackals;
   you covered us over with deep darkness.

ANYONE WHO POSSESSES EVEN the most basic knowledge about biblical faith will know that with God's covenant love comes covenant obligations. Weekly we are reminded from the pulpit that while grace is amazing, it carries demands, and woe betide the person who reneges on their commitment. What I have never heard, however, in any service of worship, is a congregant accusing God of reneging on his commitments. In public prayers one might hear petitions, and sometimes even laments, but never an accusation that God has failed to keep up his side of the deal. Yet, this is precisely what we have here in this astonishing psalm: Israel has kept her side of the deal, not strayed from the path, but God has not kept his side of the deal by upholding her in battle. But what is possibly more astonishing than the accusation of God's forgetfulness is the plea at the end for God to yet rouse himself on her behalf, to yet act according to his steadfast love. Not only does it represent a remarkable conviction about the power of prayer but, more importantly, a tenacious belief in the faithfulness of God. This final plea represents a bond of the highest order, and one that should inspire, for only intimates can call each other to account.

Prayer: *Some things, Lord, I just don't understand. Here we are trying to do our best, but most of the time we feel crushed. Even so, I am still trusting that you will put things right. Amen.*

Psalm 45

Royal

⁶ Your throne, O God, will last for ever and ever;
    a scepter of justice will be the scepter of your kingdom.
⁷ You love righteousness and hate wickedness;
    therefore God, your God, has set you above your companions
    by anointing you with the oil of joy.
⁸ All your robes are fragrant with myrrh and aloes and cassia;
    from palaces adorned with ivory
    the music of the strings makes you glad.
⁹ Daughters of kings are among your honored women;
    at your right hand is the royal bride in gold of Ophir.

THIS IS THE FOURTH in a little collection of psalms of the sons of Korah (43–49). And what a psalm it is: rhetorically unique; stylistically remarkable; a love song—an epithalamion—the kind you might find in Renaissance literature, celebrating the wedding of the king. Coming off the back of a series of laments, Psalm 45 is arguably all the more overwhelming as an evocation of love. The poet speaks as he writes, in gathering ecstasy, of the majesty of the king and the beauty of his bride. To pray this psalm is to enter into a riot of colors and scents as the two make their way to the altar. If we are not careful, we will become intoxicated by the sheer lavishness of the occasion. But to pray this psalm is also to enter into a mystery, to borrow a word from St. Paul. As we celebrate the joy of young love—the power of her beauty to arouse his desire, the strength of his majesty to command her respect—we feel that we are touching the hem of a much larger world. All the things we long for—mutuality, humility, and justice—are finally consummated. No wonder the writer to the Hebrews takes this psalm and ascribes it to the Son of God (Heb 1:8–9). This image of the bridegroom waiting for his bride is none other than a revelation of the divine.

Prayer: *Lord, I had no idea that faith in you could be so sensuous. I love it. Please keep intoxicating me with the sights and sounds and smells of your kingdom. Amen.*

Psalm 46

Zion Psalm

[9] He makes wars cease
   to the ends of the earth.
He breaks the bow and shatters the spear;
   he burns the shields with fire.
[10] He says, "Be still, and know that I am God;
   I will be exalted among the nations,
   I will be exalted in the earth."

THIS MUCH LOVED PSALM continues the hopeful tone of Psalm 45 with a celebration of God's presence in Zion. Its popularity lies in the affirmation that while everything around us is collapsing, we won't collapse because God is a mighty fortress. No matter how shaky the ground is, or how threatening our enemies, we will not fear because God is with us. The fact that his help comes at break of day is a pretty good incentive for early morning prayer, or so Bonhoeffer thought.

Two further images stick out, however, whenever we pray this psalm. The first is of a stream that brings refreshment to the city of God—even as the earth is beset by surging waters. And the second is a somewhat paradoxical image of a warrior King fighting to bring an end to all war. It is here in this second image that we hear the command to "be still and know that I am God." In truth, this is not so much a call to quietness but a declaration that God is destroying all military options. But then again, maybe the emphasis on prayerful stillness is not so wrong either. For what is silence, and even solitude but a relinquishment of fear, and the faith that no matter how noisy the earth has become, no matter how aggressive, God's voice is louder still.

Prayer: *Lord, as soon as I wake up there is so much clamoring for my attention. It feels as if the world is out of control. What a relief that at the center of all things is your steadfast love. Amen.*

Psalm 47

Enthronement

⁵ God has ascended amid shouts of joy,
    the Lᴏʀᴅ amid the sounding of trumpets.
⁶ Sing praises to God, sing praises;
    sing praises to our King, sing praises.
⁷ For God is the King of all the earth;
    sing to him a psalm of praise.

Wʜᴇɴᴇᴠᴇʀ ᴘᴇᴏᴘʟᴇ ɪɴ ᴛʜᴇ congregation complain to me about the loudness of contemporary worship, I can't help thinking of this psalm. For sure, we will never know exactly what is being described here, but we can be pretty sure it wasn't a Quaker meeting! And why not? The King has ascended on high. Not for him the merely religious spheres of our world; nor the exclusive world of the people of Israel; rather, God is the King over *all* the earth. As Abraham Kuyper famously put it with reference to the ascension of Christ: "There is not a square inch in the whole domain of our human existence over which Christ, who is Sovereign over all, does not cry *Mine*." If this doesn't raise a shout, the odd blast of a trumpet, I don't know what will. Indeed, one of the reasons there is such a din going on is because in Psalm 47 the actual enthronement of the King is being enacted. Everyone knows of course that this is already so. There is not one worshipper who does not rejoice in the fact that God is already on the throne. But in worship it's as if we are seeing it for the first time, with the express purpose of awakening wonder. Sometimes that means silence, sometimes weeping. But sometimes we simply need to raise the roof.

Prayer: *Lord, overcome my reticence, and even my quietness, and help me enter into your joy. Amen.*

Psalm 48

Zion Psalm

² Beautiful in its loftiness,
   the joy of the whole earth,
like the heights of Zaphon is Mount Zion,
   the city of the Great King.
³ God is in her citadels;
   he has shown himself to be her fortress.

IT IS DIFFICULT FOR us to understand the affection with which the city of Jerusalem was held by the psalmist—affection for the temple in particular. Put aside images of a cathedral-like building in the city; in many ways the temple was the city, and in a very real sense the place where God chose to locate his presence.

God cannot be reduced to a building of course. Whenever this starts to happen, or whenever the people presume on God's protection, regardless of obedience, he sends his prophets to denounce their idolatry. But even so, in ways that are often hard for Protestants to understand, this psalm teaches us that God loves matter. Time and place are not at odds with his being but are the expression of his love; sensuality and beauty not something to be ashamed of but celebrated. For Christians, the joy that the psalmist feels as he walks around the ramparts, wondering at God's unfailing love, finds its ultimate focus in the person of Jesus Christ. God becoming flesh is not a confidence trick—something impossible that God does anyway—but rather the natural conclusion to the story of a God whose desire is to inhabit the world he has made. With the psalmist, we should consider it well, and tell it to our children.

Prayer: *Lord, I just love to inhabit the story of your unfailing love and I just love to tell it to my children. Amen.*

Psalm 49

Wisdom

[7] No one can redeem the life of another
   or give to God a ransom for them—
[8] the ransom for a life is costly,
   no payment is ever enough—
[9] so that they should live on forever
   and not see decay.

DEATH IS NOT ONLY the grim reaper but the grim leveller. As is told in Psalm 49 (which is surely the most explicit piece of wisdom writing in the whole of the Psalter), wealth is no protection, no ransom even, against the inevitability of the grave. Even though on this earth the rich were famous, living in their impressive houses, putting their names to all kinds of things, now their habitation is under the earth in an everlasting darkness. The psalm is urging all of us in fact to grasp the ephemerality of life and not let our wealth deceive us into thinking that life goes on and on. Yes, it seems permanent, but it is in fact transient, and no amount of money can insure against it.

Before we are done praying this psalm, however, feeling convicted possibly about our riches, or at least reminded that "you cannot take it with you," there is a sense that even though money cannot redeem a life, God can. By letting go of smugness, and staying close to him, there is yet hope beyond death. What it looks like is not developed here. For that we need an empty tomb.

Prayer: *Lord, it is good to be reminded of our mortality. It keeps us humble. But it is good also to be reminded of your immortality. It keeps us hopeful. Amen.*

Psalm 50
Hymn with Prophetic Warning

⁹ I have no need of a bull from your stall
   or of goats from your pens,
¹⁰ for every animal of the forest is mine,
   and the cattle on a thousand hills.
¹¹ I know every bird in the mountains,
   and the insects in the fields are mine.
¹² If I were hungry I would not tell you,
   for the world is mine, and all that is in it.

GATHERING TOGETHER TO HEAR the word of God is generally regarded a dangerous thing to do. To be sure, it is a celebration of his gracious love, but everyone knows that covenant love also calls us to account. And here in this holy convocation of Psalm 50, everyone seated in their pews, God calls us to account on two fronts. The second is perhaps easier to identify. It is the age-old sin of hypocrisy: of saying one thing and doing another. The Lord has no truck with this kind of wickedness, and he says so in no uncertain terms. Prior to this, however, he calls to account the faithful as well. Their problem is not the sin of hypocrisy but the pride of presumption: the misguided notion that by simply performing the sacrifice they can somehow manipulate the deity. Or if not presumption, then delusion, that God somehow needs our worship. To such theological drivel, God reminds us that if he were hungry for the odd sacrifice it is not us he would turn to, because he owns everything of course. Those proverbial hills of his, thousands of them apparently, are simply laden with cattle, not to mention bulls, goats, birds—and even the tiniest insects. So rather than thinking we have a handle on God, the best thing we can do is learn to sing thankfully, call upon the Lord passionately, and, above all, make sure we walk the talk.

Prayer: *Forgive me, Lord, if I ever thought you were deficient, needful of my resources. What arrogance. It is I who need you, not you who needs me. Amen.*

Psalm 51

Individual Lament

¹⁶ You do not delight in sacrifice, or I would bring it;
you do not take pleasure in burnt offerings.
¹⁷ My sacrifice, O God, is a broken spirit;
a broken and contrite heart
you, God, will not despise.

ACCORDING TO THE HEADLINE, Psalm 51 was written by David when the prophet Nathan came to him after David had committed adultery with Bathsheba. In our desire to get to the psalm itself we can miss the significance of this superscription because the truth is that court prophets don't usually survive such initiatives. Nathan's courage in telling a parable in order to expose David's crime was more likely to end with his head chopped off than with a psalm. To David's credit, however, when Nathan had finished his tale, skillfully exposing the king's greed, he more than answered the prophet's finger-pointing "Thou art the man," with a simple: "I have sinned against the LORD." No attempt to cover up; no pleading mitigating circumstances; just a straightforward confession and a heartfelt cry for mercy.

Strange as it sounds, maybe Psalm 51 is one of the reasons why David is known as a man after God's own heart. After all, holiness is not the ability to pretend a perfect life but rather the willingness to face the residual darkness in our hearts, to bring it all before God, and then experience the renewing grace of the Holy Spirit. In terms of sanctification it doesn't seem very much; and in terms of penitence it doesn't sound very impressive at all. More impressive, for us at least, would be a lavish sacrifice, with all the trimmings. More precious to God, however, and something he will never spurn, is the sacrifice of a broken and contrite heart.

Prayer: *It is hard for me to believe, but I will try to anyway, that just now it is my broken and penitent heart that draws you to me. Amen.*

Psalm 52

Individual Lament

⁸ But I am like an olive tree
     flourishing in the house of God;
I trust in God's unfailing love
     for ever and ever.
⁹ For what you have done I will always praise you
     in the presence of your faithful people.
And I will hope in your name,
     for your name is good.

EVERY NOW AND THEN we come across a genuinely evil person: someone who seems intent on destroying others in order to get on. As far as David was concerned, Doeg the Edomite was one such person. He is the archetypal villain who exploits David's misfortune for his own ends, ingratiating himself with King Saul by informing him of David's whereabouts, and then, if that is not enough, committing sacrilege by killing the priests of Nob.

We need places to deal with our hatred of these people. Psalm 52 is one such place. By praying this psalm we can express our sheer loathing of these big shots as well as join in the laughter of the righteous who are privy to their fall. Whether their demise will be realized in the short term we don't know. The Doegs of this world have an incredible ability to survive. Even so, it is good to express in prayer what we think of them, and then remind ourselves that there is a future for one who trusts in God. Unlike the wicked who will one day get uprooted from their self-made lives, those who hope in God are rooted like a verdant olive tree. This is the reason the psalmist ends up praising God, for in the end good will triumph.

Prayer: *I am sorry, Lord, that I have been ranting on about the wicked. To be honest, it is good to get it off my chest. Now I can trust in you again, for your name is good. Amen.*

Psalm 53
Community Lament

⁴ Do all these evildoers know nothing?
They devour my people as though eating bread;
   they never call on God.
⁵ But there they are, overwhelmed with dread,
   where there was nothing to dread.
God scattered the bones of those who attacked you;
   you put them to shame, for God despised them.

IT'S A BIT DISCONCERTING in some ways to find Psalm 14 repeated here in Psalm 53, although anyone familiar with the Gospels will know that duplications are commonplace. In each instance they can add something new to the canon of scripture. For example, the cleansing of the temple episode comes at the beginning of John's Gospel and not, as with the Synoptics, toward the end. John's decision to place it there is unusual, if not problematic, but it strengthens what he wants to say in those opening chapters about organized religion.

Something similar in terms of sequencing is going on here. It might help us to notice that Psalm 53 is preceded, as we have just seen, by a psalm where the demise of the wicked is celebrated. Hence, the editor of Book II places a repeat of Psalm 14 here in this next psalm (effectively Psalm 53) and tweaks it in such a way as to reinforce this theme. If v. 6 of Psalm 14 emphasizes God's refuge for the righteous, v. 6 of Psalm 53 emphasizes God's ruination of the wicked, and thus strengthens the theme begun in Psalm 52 with the attack upon Doeg. It's not much, I know. In terms of liturgy, why not write a brand new psalm? Even so, it works. And the fact that it is also set to a different tune to that of Psalm 14 reminds us that in the end psalms are meant to be sung rather than studied.

Prayer: *Sometimes, Lord, this prayer book feels a little dog-eared. It feels almost thrown together. But actually I love it. These prayers are as fresh as anything I know. Amen.*

Psalm 54
Individual Lament

⁴ Surely God is my help;
  the Lord is the one who sustains me.
⁵ Let evil recoil on those who slander me;
  in your faithfulness destroy them.
⁶ I will sacrifice a freewill offering to you;
  I will praise your name, LORD, for it is good.
⁷ You have delivered me from all my troubles,
  and my eyes have looked in triumph on my foes.

IT MIGHT BE WORTH reminding ourselves as we continue through the Psalter that for all the therapeutic value of these prayers, and for all the meditative joy in speaking them out, in the end prayer is petition. There's no point getting all snooty about this. Prayer in its purest form is beseeching God to get us out of a hole. As C. S. Lewis once said: "I only pray when I'm in trouble, but since I'm in trouble a lot, I pray a lot." And in Psalm 54 we have a short but sweet model of how we might pray, as well as what we might expect, because the answers are almost immediate. No sooner has David prayed for help, God comes to his aid. In the short space of a *selah,* the psalm moves from a desert lament to a song of thanksgiving. It's as if God knows what we need before we even ask, and delivers with surprising speed. So it is good to pray this psalm; although it has to be said that if one was asked to draw up a list of favorite psalms, I doubt Psalm 54 would make anyone's top ten. Compared to Psalm 23, for example, it is relatively unknown. Compared to other psalms of lament, say Psalm 42, or Psalm 139, it is quite sprightly. But maybe this is what the poet George Herbert was on about when he referred to prayer as "reversed thunder." In a word, prayer is powerful.

Prayer: *I don't mind praying long, persistent prayers to you, Lord. I am willing to wait. But I also love it when you answer quickly. Thank you. Amen.*

Psalm 55

Individual Lament

⁶ I said, "Oh, that I had the wings of a dove!
  I would fly away and be at rest.
⁷ I would flee far away
  and stay in the desert;
⁸ I would hurry to my place of shelter,
  far from the tempest and storm."

ONE OF THE REASONS why the Psalms are universally popular is because although they arise from ancient settings they feel like our world. The violence that patrols the walls of the city here in Psalm 55 could as well be said of any modern city. And who has not cried "O for the wings of a dove" in order to escape the corruption? Pretty much everyone. The only problem is that God has not given us wings. Last time I looked there were just a couple of arms attached to my side. So presumably he intends us to stay put and work out a way of surviving where we are. Indeed, the rest of Psalm 55 is a journey toward that very place where finally, despite everything that has happened, we can cast our cares upon the Lord because we know that he will sustain us. But if we think this is a straightforward journey, praying this psalm reminds us that the route from fear to trust is often a tortuous one. In fact, there are times when it is not entirely clear who the psalmist is speaking with. Sometimes it is God, other times himself, and then still other times it appears he is addressing his betrayer directly, only then to conclude with some kind of exhortation to an imaginary congregation. Which all goes to say that prayer is often quite random; and psalms are condensed compilations of what in reality are long, wandering prayers. We should not regard this rambling, or even rawness, as an enemy to prayer, but rather its essence.

Prayer: *Thank you, Lord, that for all meanderings of my disconcerted soul finally you bring me to the place where I can lay everything at your feet. Amen.*

Psalm 56

Individual Lament

⁸ Record my misery;
  list my tears on your scroll—
  are they not in your record?
⁹ Then my enemies will turn back
  when I call for help.
  By this I will know that God is for me.

"REAL MEN DON'T CRY," they say. "Tears are a sign of weakness." Well, you can't get a more real man than David, nor anyone stronger. He became the most powerful and most celebrated king Israel ever had. Yet, David unashamedly speaks of times in his life—like here in Philistine territory— when he wept. Indeed, I can't think of a single hero of the faith whose tears have not been essential to the unfolding of their story. Even the great Augustine talks on one occasion in *The Confessions* about his tears flowing freely, making a pillow for his broken heart. What is so striking about David's tears, however, is that they ended up not on his pillow but in God's specially made flask. Tenderly, God collected them, counting each one into his bottle as a testimony to David's troubled soul. This is not so much a striking image but a scandalous one for it presents to us not the God of all power but the God of all grief, who feels our sorrow.

It makes a difference of course to know that God registers our grief. Like when we confide in a friend and find we can't stop crying. Their treasuring of our weeping is the moment of transformation—remarkably so. As the tears stream down his face, God attempting to bottle each one, David's fears morph into faith, his enemies now a footnote, not a threat.

Prayer: *Thank you, Lord, that my tears are not a hindrance to receiving your love but the place where your love is made most real. Amen.*

Psalm 57

Individual Lament

⁷ My heart, O God, is steadfast,
   my heart is steadfast;
   I will sing and make music.
⁸ Awake, my soul!
   Awake, harp and lyre!
   I will awaken the dawn.

IT WAS DIETRICH BONHOEFFER who said "the early morning belongs to the church of the Risen Christ." He is right of course. Early on the first day of the week, while it was still dark, Mary Magdalene stumbled on the brightness of an empty tomb. As a devotee of the Psalms, Bonhoeffer knew, however, that the notion of the early morning as a time of God's special favor is not only rooted in the resurrection but anticipated in the prayers of Israel. As expressed here in Psalm 57, the morning is a time of deliverance, so the psalmist will wake early with his harp and lyre in order to praise and thank God for it. A bit like in the film *Black Orpheus*, where the hero Orpheus convinces the two little boys that his guitar playing makes the sun come up in the morning, there is a sense in this psalm that our waking invokes God's saving. And it's not that God ceases to be a refuge and a shelter once the morning passes. Not at all. The rousing of the dawn at the eastern edge of the world leads the psalmist at the end to exalt in God over all the heavens. But maybe there is something about these early hours that freshens up God's mercies, makes them new, and sends them to our address. As the hymn writer puts it: "Great is thy faithfulness, Great is thy faithfulness. Morning by morning new mercies I see."

Prayer: *I do believe, dear Lord, there is such a thing as rising early for the love of God. Thank you for this special grace that exists in the half-light of the dawn. Amen.*

Psalm 58

Community Lament

⁶ Break the teeth in their mouths, O God;
  LORD, tear out the fangs of those lions!
⁷ Let them vanish like water that flows away;
  when they draw the bow, let their arrows fall short.
⁸ May they be like a slug that melts away as it moves along,
  like a stillborn child that never sees the sun.

IT'S ONE OF THOSE psalms again. In technical language we call it an impreca-
tion; in actuality, we consider it language you wouldn't want your Grandma
to hear. My goodness me! This is the stuff of football terraces, not worship
services. But there it is: Psalm 58. A place all of its own in the Psalter. It's
important to note, however, without in anyway detracting from the vulgar-
ity of the images, that these are not curses upon the wicked but prayers
unto God. And what they are crying out for is not vengeance but justice. In
fact, the psalmist is doing exactly what we are supposed to do when we feel
overwhelmed by the corruption in the world: that is, entrust everything to
God. After all, "vengeance is mine" says the Lord (Rom 12:19). And to pray
for the vengeance of God is to pray that his justice will be carried out. And
if, having said all that, we still have a problem with this prayer, then we have
a problem with being holy, for holiness is not the absence of anger but its
expression in the face of intolerable evil: those venomous snakes who turn
a deaf ear to the cries of the poor. In fact, to not get angry over this kind
of societal injustice is a sin in itself. It is to collude with the powers that be
rather than pray "your kingdom come."

Prayer: *What a relief that I can bring everything to you, even my indignation.*
What you do about it, Lord, is your business, but at least you know how I feel.
Amen.

Psalm 59
Individual Lament

⁹ You are my strength, I watch for you;
   you, God, are my fortress,
¹⁰   my God on whom I can rely.
God will go before me
   and will let me gloat over those who slander me.
¹¹ But do not kill them, Lord our shield,
   or my people will forget.
In your might uproot them
   and bring them down.

ANOTHER PSALM OF LAMENT, and with a particularly vindictive request that God does not totally kill David's enemies but leave them to totter, so he might have the pleasure of watching them squirm. It's not a very pleasant thought, but who hasn't entertained it? I can recall many movies where I have wanted exactly that; and I can think of a few real-life situations as well, I'm ashamed to say, where I have relished the prospect of gloating over the demise of the proud. The whole point of these psalms, however, is to not feel ashamed but rather to own the thought and bring it to God. Put it this way: better to pray it than to enact it. Furthermore, since no secrets are hid from him, to pray the psalm is only to say what God already knows. Above all, however, Psalm 59 teaches us that by praying our vindictiveness it is possible to get to a place where we exhaust our anger and learn instead to trust. Certainly that's what happened to David. Saul sent men to watch David's house, but David learnt to watch for God. In watching, he discovers that he can totally rely on God's strength to keep him. Though his enemies prowl around the city like dogs, he finds God to be a fortress. What looks on the surface like a psalm full of curses turns out to be a psalm full of faith.

Prayer: *Thank you, Lord, that through all the contortions of my heart you turn my introspection and my anger into trust and praise. Amen.*

Psalm 60
Community Lament

⁶ God has spoken from his sanctuary:
   "In triumph I will parcel out Shechem
   and measure off the Valley of Sukkoth.
⁷ Gilead is mine, and Manasseh is mine;
   Ephraim is my helmet,
   Judah is my scepter.
⁸ Moab is my washbasin,
   on Edom I toss my sandal;
   over Philistia I shout in triumph."

THEY SAY HISTORY IS written by the victors. The same could be said of some of the Psalms. In all likelihood Psalm 60 only makes the canon because David's prayer for success in battle was actually answered. Somewhere between v. 5 and v. 6—in the pregnancy between prayer and response—a miracle takes place, so that what began as collective despair turns into national victory, and then ends up as a song. Coming after a whole sequence of laments, this victory shout is a welcome reprieve of course, although it is important to note that what David celebrates here on the mountain top is precisely the same as that which he celebrates in the wilderness: namely the faithfulness of God. No mention of military strategy; no gory details of battle; no self-preening now that he is triumphant; just utter reliance on the Lord for the successes he gives. In an age like ours where there are deep sensitivities around the combination of religion and violence, the contempt David expresses over Moab, Edom, and Philistia might make us feel uncomfortable. It smacks of fundamentalism. What is undeniable, however, is that there is nothing abstract about Israel's faith—or ours. Geography matters. Our banner is not some abstract idea but exodus, Zion, and Calvary.

Prayer: *Lord, I thank you for the times when I am in despair for they remind me that I am at all times and in all places utterly dependant on you. Amen.*

Psalm 61
Individual Lament

^{2} From the ends of the earth I call to you,
  I call as my heart grows faint;
  lead me to the rock that is higher than I.
^{3} For you have been my refuge,
  a strong tower against the foe.
^{4} I long to dwell in your tent forever
  and take refuge in the shelter of your wings.
^{5} For you, God, have heard my vows;
  you have given me the heritage of those who fear your name.

LIFE IS CHAOTIC. SOMETIMES it can feel overwhelming. Circumstances conspire so that it feels as if we are barely keeping our head above the water. It's a relief to know, therefore, that there is a place we can go when things get like that—a rock that sits above the rising waters, and which will keep us safe until the torrent has passed. For the psalmist, this place is the temple. There, in front of the altar of God, under the wings of the cherubim, is the sanctuary that the human heart longs for. Prayer is all about coming under its refuge. Indeed, I wonder sometimes if prayer is really just a hankering for this sacred canopy. After all, if the Psalms are anything to go by, the times when things just go swimmingly well are few and far between. Most times we feel like we are living on the edge—at "the ends of the earth!" So what prayer is, in its most basic form, is a cry for the tented center, for the covering of God's protecting love. That David makes a vow to thank God, should God answer his cry, is not as manipulative as it sounds. It's actually a statement of faith, for David knows, perhaps like no one else, that what begins as a plea will likely end in praise.

Prayer: *Lord, there is nothing better than coming under the canopy of your love. I am so grateful to you that such a shelter exists. Amen.*

Psalm 62
Individual Lament

⁵ Yes, my soul, find rest in God;
   my hope comes from him.
⁶ Truly he is my rock and my salvation;
   he is my fortress, I will not be shaken.
⁷ My salvation and my honor depend on God;
   he is my mighty rock, my refuge.
⁸ Trust in him at all times, you people;
   pour out your hearts to him,
   for God is our refuge.

RESTLESSNESS SEEMS TO BE the chronic condition of the soul. Typically, in an attempt to cure it, we try to cram as much as we can into our schedule. We hope that by climbing up the ladder we will somehow assuage our demons. But as much as wealth and ambition promise to save, they can do nothing of the kind. In truth, they often make things worse. Only in God, says the psalmist, is my being quiet. So much does David believe this that he speaks the refrain to himself a number of times, and on one occasion even turns it into a command: "Only in God, quiet my soul" (Robert Alter's translation). On another occasion he speaks wisdom, reminding himself that the reason "God only" is our refuge is because we only are a breath. The heart of this psalm reminds me of the opening chapter of *The Confessions* where Augustine says; "You have made us for yourself O Lord and our hearts are restless until they find their rest in thee." Once we find this place, the psalm assures us that nothing can shake us from it, not even personal attacks. Whilst those who trust in riches get more and more agitated, often meting out their anger on the innocent, the one who trusts in God will rest secure, because they will be living close to the center.

Prayer: *Teach me, Lord, amidst all the distractedness of our world to do the one thing needful. Amen.*

Psalm 63

Individual Lament

² I have seen you in the sanctuary
　and beheld your power and your glory.
³ Because your love is better than life,
　my lips will glorify you.
⁴ I will praise you as long as I live,
　and in your name I will lift up my hands.
⁵ I will be fully satisfied as with the richest of foods;
　with singing lips my mouth will praise you.

WE REMEMBER DAVID AS a king, but much of his life was formed in the wilderness. Stripped of all the props of civilization, away from the centers of worship, his faith took on the nature of raw desire: a longing that rivals the yearning between lovers; a love that is better than life itself. It's as if the desert had become his inner landscape, generating a deep thirst for God. As Augustine prayed: "Thou hast put salt on our lips so that we might thirst for thee."

As David's prayer continues, the sensuality of these opening verses intensifies. And it becomes a study in contrasts. At the end of the psalm we read that the mouths of liars will be stopped. Those who seek David's life will be left as food for the jackals (surely the worst shame that can befall a dead body); whereas for David, having a love for God is by definition to have an open mouth. After all, it is with our mouths that we praise him, and with our mouths that we feast at his table. Indeed, it seems clear enough that an open mouth is in fact an open heart—and one that remains open even in the darkness. For even though the sanctuary is far away, and even though the desert nights are full of danger, an open heart can conjure up shadows of God.

Prayer: *Lord, we do indeed live in a dry and a weary land. Thank you that you satisfy our longings, again and again. Amen.*

Psalm 64

Individual Lament

⁷ But God will shoot them with his arrows;
  they will suddenly be struck down.
⁸ He will turn their own tongues against them
  and bring them to ruin;
  all who see them will shake their heads in scorn.
⁹ All people will fear;
  they will proclaim the works of God
  and ponder what he has done.

"STICKS AND STONES WILL break my bones but names will never hurt me." Really? Not according to this psalm. Verbal attacks are incredibly painful. The very reason the psalmist voices a complaint to God is precisely because the gossip and slander he has been subject to has proven so deadly—like slings and arrows into our unfortunate hearts. In short, malicious words have the power to totally wreck lives. But prayer is powerful also. More powerful. As a result of praying to God, the arrows meant for us land on the wicked instead; evil words boomerang and bring about ruin; and what was devised in secret, beyond finding out, ends up in public, seen by all. In fact, you could say that prayer creates the most wonderful ironies. Again, the issue is not vengeance. Psalm 64 does not conclude with us rubbing our hands in glee at the demise of the proud but rather thanking God that there is justice in the world after all. And what could be more beneficent than thankful words?

Prayer: *I cannot deny, Lord, that I feel good when I see justice in the world. It reminds me that you are in charge after all. Amen.*

Psalm 65

Creation

⁹ You care for the land and water it;
   you enrich it abundantly.
The streams of God are filled with water
   to provide the people with grain,
   for so you have ordained it.
¹⁰ You drench its furrows and level its ridges;
   you soften it with showers and bless its crops.
¹¹ You crown the year with your bounty,
   and your carts overflow with abundance.

How EASY IT IS for our thoughts about redemption to be separated from our theology of creation. It happens all the time in religious communities. We sing "ransomed, healed, restored, forgiven," but rather than going on to rejoice in the grand vistas "of the ends of the earth" we retreat instead into a spiritual cul-de-sac of private pieties. In worst case scenarios we end up inhabiting a "parallel" and sometimes even a "paranoid" universe. Psalm 65, however, permits no such divergence. The God who saves is the God who has created this whole thing. No sooner does the psalmist celebrate the forgiveness of sins, than he's over the seas and across the mountains, finding his way around God's big country. Indeed, as much as it is true that even "silence is praise" (Robert Alter's translation of v. 1), it's not one verse later that the psalmist is simply bursting into song at the sheer wonder of God's creation. And with "rinsed eyes," to use Merton's description of a faith-filled life, everything takes on the nature of gift. The rains are showers of blessings; the rivers are streams of God; and the hills are attired with the flocks of heaven. This is worship on a grand scale. Not the narrowing of faith to the neurosis of the soul but an expansion of faith to the majesties of the earth.

Prayer: *O Lord, deliver me from sour-faced, narrow-minded religion, and immerse me instead in the grand sweep of your redeemed creation. Amen.*

Psalm 66
Individual Psalm of Thanksgiving

⁵ Come and see what God has done,
  his awesome deeds for mankind!
⁶ He turned the sea into dry land,
  they passed through the waters on foot—
  come, let us rejoice in him.
⁷ He rules forever by his power,
  his eyes watch the nations—
  let not the rebellious rise up against him.

IT IS A STRIKING if not scandalous feature of our faith that the God we worship is a God who has revealed himself in time, space, and history. He is not God in the abstract but God as he has acted in the affairs of his people, the exodus being the original miracle. Psalm 66 celebrates this. It recounts the parting of the sea, the coming out from the yoke of slavery, and the arrival into a spacious freedom. In fact, praise is not praise unless it has this powerful rescue—this awesome deed—somewhere as its theme. We do not indulge in philosophical enquiries into the being of God but rather in songs of praise to the God who acts. As scandalous as it sounds, we also rejoice that this particular God, who has acted in this particular way, with this particular people, is the God of the whole earth.

At some point or other of course prayer must become personal—which it does here in Psalm 66. The great climatic miracle of exodus becomes the originator of all miracles that come to us as a result of prayer. But if we ever thought prayer was simply a matter of technique, this psalm reminds us it is all about truth. God can put up with us not saying the exact right words; what he cannot endure is our hiding sin in our hearts.

Prayer: *Thank you, Lord, that through all the trials and tribulations of this life you are refining me to be pure silver. Amen.*

68

Psalm 67
Community Psalm of Thanksgiving

¹ May God be gracious to us and bless us
  and make his face shine on us—
² so that your ways may be known on earth,
  your salvation among all nations.

FOR ALL OUR CONCERNS about the prosperity gospel—the way it legitimizes greed and self-centeredness—the truth of the matter is that God wants to prosper us. The desire to bless his people lies right at the heart of the Abrahamic covenant. By the time we get to Moses it ritualizes into what must surely be the most enticing image of blessedness ever: the face of God. The Lord bless you and keep you. The Lord make his face shine upon you.

Incidentally, if we think that this Aaronic blessing represents the spiritualization of land—the translation of real estate into liturgy—we are mistaken. Psalm 67 makes it clear that the blessing is unashamedly material. When God shines his face, as opposed to hides his face, we are talking harvests, not just holiness. But if we think that the blessing is only to his chosen we are similarly mistaken because the heart of the psalm is all about nations. It always has been. A gospel for all nations is not alien to the promise but its inevitable climax. Abram becomes Abraham because "all nations will be blessed through you," says the Lord. Whatever God does for his people, whatever blessing we receive, it is as well for us to remember that it is so that the "ends of the earth may fear him."

Prayer: *Lord, you are exclusive in your deity, yet abundant in your generosity. I praise you that you renege on neither in the way you rule your creation. Amen.*

Psalm 68
General Hymn

¹⁷ The chariots of God are tens of thousands
  and thousands of thousands;
   the Lord has come from Sinai into his sanctuary.
¹⁸ When you ascended on high,
  you took many captives;
  you received gifts from people,
even from the rebellious—
  that you, LORD God, might dwell there.

GOSPEL MEANS GLAD TIDINGS. It has the feel of an announcement. Something tremendous has happened and news of it needs to get out. Be it a company of preachers or a band of musicians, the world needs to know the shout of the King. Psalm 68 recounts this. From Sinai, through the wilderness, and on to Zion, it is unashamedly triumphant. In contrast to many other psalms which play the minor key, this psalm completes a flurry of four psalms that revel in the victory of God—thus confirming to us that a hymn book needs the whole array of worship songs if it is to be of use to the people of God. As James Stewart notes concerning a similar period in Israel's history, and then in relation to the ascension of Christ: "it is true that Christ is the servant Messiah, the 'man for others.' But it is also true that God has given him the kingdom and the cosmic dimension, and on his head are many crowns." For all our antipathy to triumphalism, to not have this note of triumph at the heart of our processions is to dishonor that little tribe of Benjamin leading the great throng. It is to deny the uniqueness of our faith and its particular mission to the poor of our world. Put it like this: if the widows and orphans sing for joy, then so should we. As the psalm concludes: Praise be to God!

Prayer: *Help me, Lord, never to lose sight of your victory. For all the fellowship of your suffering, keep before me the power of your resurrection. Amen.*

Psalm 69
Individual Lament

[19] You know how I am scorned, disgraced, and shamed;
  all my enemies are before you.
[20] Scorn has broken my heart
  and has left me helpless;
I looked for sympathy, but there was none,
  for comforters, but I found none.
[21] They put gall in my food
  and gave me vinegar for my thirst.

IN AN AGE OF mediocrity and cultural conformity, passionate faith will always stand out as a bit mad. Furthermore, anyone who has the courage to actually challenge the *status quo* runs the serious risk of getting killed. It seems to be an occupational hazard of all prophetic people. In this respect, as we pray through Psalm 69 our minds may well wander back to the story of Jeremiah: his courage in speaking out against corruption, his isolation as the people reject his message, and his complaint that God should ever have laid this burden upon him. Or we may simply jump ahead to the passion of Jesus. After all, the Gospel writers quote from this psalm a few times, incorporating into the crucifixion itself the tiny detail of vinegar that was offered to quench his thirst. Is it that Jesus fulfilled these prophesies directly, or is it that when the Gospel writers came to reflect upon the ministry of Jesus they couldn't help but cast him in the role of the righteous sufferer of Psalm 69? Either way, the crucifixion is an apt commentary on Psalm 69, a telling echo of the ministry of Jeremiah, and a great encouragement to anyone who is experiencing the splinters of going against the grain.

Prayer: *I don't understand, Lord, why some people find my message so offensive. It seems like good news to me. But since they are offended, help me to bring the pain of rejection to you. Amen.*

Psalm 70
Individual Lament

⁵ But as for me, I am poor and needy;
   come quickly to me, O God.
You are my help and my deliverer;
   LORD, do not delay.

SOMETIMES WHEN WE PRAY we make the mistake of thinking that the longer we pray the more impressed God will be. It's not so much that we want to be showy but that we want to be deep, and say things in a way that at least sounds spiritual. Psalm 70 is there to remind us that sometimes a short, sharp, urgent prayer is all that is needed. In fact, Psalm 70 is such a brief prayer that I have heard it described as a sigh. But that's the point: sometimes, if not most times, a sigh is enough. Not only is it all we can muster; it is all that is needed to capture God's attention. The urgency of the request, the desperate need for help, the cry for vindication, and the desire to see things resolved quickly, is the stuff of prayer, and the very thing that elicits God's mercy.

We have already prayed this prayer, of course. It featured almost verbatim toward the end of Psalm 40. My guess, however, is that what we have here in Psalm 70 is the original prayer. In my opinion, Psalm 70 was not spliced off Psalm 40 but rather was attached to the end of Psalm 40, mainly for its note of urgency. In other words, it is a prayer in its own right. In no way should we dismiss it as a lesser prayer because of its brevity; rather we should regard it as the very height of prayer.

Prayer: *It's good to know, Lord, that you don't require long, well-constructed prayers before you answer us. Since you know all things, a sigh is enough for you. Amen.*

Psalm 71

Individual Lament

¹⁷ Since my youth, God, you have taught me,
   and to this day I declare your marvelous deeds.
¹⁸ Even when I am old and gray,
   do not forsake me, my God,
till I declare your power to the next generation,
   your mighty acts to all who are to come.

No one really knows what to do with illness, even more so ageing. Actually, there is a tendency in religious communities—though no one really admits to it—to regard illness and ageing with a certain degree of derision. Certainly in Psalm 71 there is a sense in which the psalmist has been made to feel isolated as a result of his growing frailty—forsaken even, as he approaches his latter years.

It's not just old age of course that can make one feel vulnerable. There are many other situations in life that can place us at the margins. But it is worth taking note that we have a whole psalm here devoted to the very real anxieties that begin to accrue with the onset of gray hair. We laugh about it, but the fears can be very real. As with all psalms, however, not only are the fears real, the prayers are real also. Moving between petition and trust, we remember that God has been there since our birth. We recall the dark nights of the soul, and the way God sustained us through it. And we rehearse the promise that the God who was midwife at our beginning will not forsake us now, but give us grace to finish well.

Prayer: *Lord, I don't like getting old. It seems like everyone forgets you. But I thank you that you don't forget me. You keep me vibrant until the end. Amen.*

Psalm 72

Royal

⁴ May he defend the afflicted among the people
　　and save the children of the needy;
　　may he crush the oppressor.
⁵ May he endure as long as the sun,
　　as long as the moon, through all generations.
⁶ May he be like rain falling on a mown field,
　　like showers watering the earth.
⁷ In his days may the righteous flourish
　　and prosperity abound till the moon is no more.

WE LONG FOR LEADERS who will rule well. In a world where power so often corrupts, and absolute power corrupts absolutely, the great cry is for leaders who will rule with justice, take pity on the weak, and rescue the needy. As we conclude Book II of the Psalms, we listen in on David's prayers for Solomon to rule in such a way. For all its idealism, and sometimes fantastical images of prosperity, David agrees that the greatness of the king is seen in how he treats the least. He also knows the ancient wisdom that while oppression lays bare the land, compassion leads to fecundity. The sound of rain falling on a mown field, of showers watering the earth, is actually the sound of love. Jesus announced something similar in his own royal manifesto. In ways that Solomon could not possibly attain, Jesus' good news to the poor was all about human flourishing. And it is this, perhaps more than anything else, that marks him out as le Roi-Soleil, the true Son of David. He rules to the ends of the earth, to be sure, but his heart is to bless. As the hymn writer puts it, and as the second book of Psalms concludes: "Let the Amen sound from His people again; gladly for aye we adore Him."

Prayer: *I couldn't imagine worshipping a King other than you, Lord. Rather than rule us with a rod of iron you serve us with gentleness and love. Amen.*

Book III

Psalm 73
Wisdom

¹⁵ If I had spoken out like that,
   I would have betrayed your children.
¹⁶ When I tried to understand all this,
   it troubled me deeply
¹⁷ till I entered the sanctuary of God;
   then I understood their final destiny.

THERE IS SOMETHING INCREDIBLY powerful about gathering to worship. At one level it is an utterly useless activity. Nothing is achieved. According to the psalmist, however, entering the sanctuary is a most energizing experience. For it is only when we are among the people of God, in the presence of God, that things begin to make sense. Up to that point, everything seems the wrong way round. Contrary to received wisdom, the wicked prosper and the righteous suffer. The suffering is so intense that one is tempted to pack it all in. What's the point of preserving a moral conscience when vanity is the order of the day? In worship, however, the celebrity culture is exposed for the illusion that it is. In the sanctuary of God everything becomes clear. Yes, you can gain the whole world, but you will lose your soul. And soul is everything.

It is good this psalm is here. As the opening psalm to Book III, it poses ultimate questions. We need to be able to do that. But whereas it starts by doubting the goodness of God, it ends by realizing that God has never actually left our side. It is not extensive reading that has brought about this transformation, or some debate about the existence of God, but the simple act of gathering together with the people of God in worship.

Prayer: *Lord, almost every time I enter your sanctuary feeling downcast, I come away with a renewed sense that actually you have never left me. Thank you. Amen.*

Psalm 74

Community Lament

¹³ It was you who split open the sea by your power;
  you broke the heads of the monster in the waters.
¹⁴ It was you who crushed the heads of Leviathan
  and gave it as food to the creatures of the desert.
¹⁵ It was you who opened up springs and streams;
  you dried up the ever-flowing rivers.
¹⁶ The day is yours, and yours also the night;
  you established the sun and moon.
¹⁷ It was you who set all the boundaries of the earth;
  you made both summer and winter.

IF, AS WE DISCOVERED in Psalm 73, the temple is the place of divine encounter, then its destruction, as recorded in Psalm 74, is not simply an architectural tragedy but a theological catastrophe. As the psalmist walks among the ruins, lamenting the sacrilegious rout of the city, it feels as if God has completely abandoned them. Yet, as so often in the Psalter, the place of utter despair is also the place of urgent prayer. There's nothing like a good ruin to arouse the compassion of God. Furthermore, if God can bring order out of chaos—separate night from day—then surely he can rescue the city. It's just a question of insistence: of throwing God's promises in his face, and forcing his hand. As we pray for God to remember his covenant, to protect his little dove from the wild beasts, one cannot help think of another catastrophe when the world returned to a watery chaos. Just as God remembered Noah, so God's remembering now brings hope out of crisis.

Prayer: *Dear Lord, just when I think everything is in chaos and about to collapse, you remind me that everything is in order. Thank you that you hold the very rhythms of life. Amen.*

Psalm 75
Community Psalm of Thanksgiving

⁶ No one from the east or the west
　or from the desert can exalt themselves.
⁷ It is God who judges:
　He brings one down, he exalts another.
⁸ In the hand of the LORD is a cup
　full of foaming wine mixed with spices;
he pours it out, and all the wicked of the earth
　drink it down to its very dregs.

THERE IS NOTHING MORE odious to God than arrogance. Strutting one's stuff may be impressive in the eyes of world but in God's sight it is detestable. It betrays a self-sufficiency that is not only ugly but stupid for it presumes a power that only God can possibly wield. In this third psalm of Book III, Asaph continues the theme of justice started in Psalm 73, and serves notice in his prayer on those who have become haughty, who raise their horn to the heavens. It is a warning that Jesus himself serves to his own generation: "He who exalts himself will be humbled," Jesus says, whereas "he who humbles himself will be exalted."

This is not the only image of course that Jesus picks up from this psalm. As well as the horn that is raised up there is the cup that is poured out. But whereas in the psalm the cup of judgment is drunk by the wicked, in Gethsemane it is Jesus himself who drinks it to the very dregs. Despite the protestations of his heart, he takes what is ours so that we receive what is his. And in this way the cup of wrath becomes the cup of mercy.

Prayer: *Help me, O God, in this world of astonishing arrogance to stay in humble dependence on you, the Servant King. Amen.*

Psalm 76

Zion Psalm

⁷ It is you alone who are to be feared.
    Who can stand before you when you are angry?
⁸ From heaven you pronounced judgment,
    and the land feared and was quiet—
⁹ when you, God, rose up to judge,
    to save all the afflicted of the land.
¹⁰ Surely your wrath against mankind brings you praise,
    and the survivors of your wrath are restrained.

IT IS POSSIBLE OVER a period of time to get overfamiliar with God. Hanging around the precincts of faith we can forget who it is we have come to worship. Psalm 76 shatters our complacency by presenting to us the fury of God. Like Mr. Beaver says to Susan when she enquiries as to the nature of Aslan, the lion: "'Safe?' said Mr. Beaver. 'Who said anything about safe? Course he isn't safe.'" Actually, according to the psalmist, he is mightier than the lions that roam the mountains. Yet, even as the psalmist describes the wildness of God, he never loses sight of the goodness of God. In fact, the only reason God gets angry is because he desires to crush the oppressors and rescue the poor. Likewise, the only reason he goes to war is to secure peace. Such is the divine economy in these matters that even human beings in the full flow of their fury will praise God for exercising the mere residue of his. Even the vanquished recognize justice when they see it. Again, in the words of Mr. Beaver: "Course he isn't safe. But he's good. He's the King, I tell you."

Prayer: *Forgive me, Lord, if I have ever got so familiar with you that I have forgotten how passionate you are about justice and righteousness. Amen.*

Psalm 77

Individual Lament

7 "Will the Lord reject forever?
  Will he never show his favor again?
8 Has his unfailing love vanished forever?
  Has his promise failed for all time?
9 Has God forgotten to be merciful?
  Has he in anger withheld his compassion?"
10 Then I thought, "To this I will appeal:
  the years when the Most High stretched out his right hand.

WE DON'T KNOW WHAT it was that caused the psalmist to pray this complaint. But whatever it was, it left him completely turned in on himself. The plethora of pronouns in the first person singular evince not only massive introspection but also chronic insomnia as the speaker goes over in his mind the good old days when nights were not broken by worry but taken up with song. What follows is a kind of anti-catechism. The questions posed are near blasphemous. They suggest that God has changed his mind about caring for his people. And yet, for all their exaggerated self-pity they act as a kind of precursor to faith because the next thing we see is the psalmist shifting from the first person to a whole series of second person pronouns. Out of sheer desperation he does what all effective prayer eventually does, even if sometimes it takes a while to get there, which is get over himself and turn instead to God. Strangely, in the memory of God's mighty acts—in the parting of seas and great thunderclaps of lightning—he goes back to sleep, secure in the shepherd's care.

Prayer: *Dear Lord, I am sorry that I exaggerate so. Help me to stop obsessing about myself and start trusting in you. Amen.*

Psalm 78

Wisdom

[70] He chose David his servant
   and took him from the sheep pens;
[71] from tending the sheep he brought him
   to be the shepherd of his people Jacob,
   of Israel his inheritance.
[72] And David shepherded them with integrity of heart;
   with skillful hands he led them.

ONE OF THE REASONS we teach history to our children is in order for them to learn from the past. Whether it is effective or not is debatable. As someone once said, one of the things we learn from history is that we learn nothing from history. Even so, the simple thing of telling one's history is well-nigh universal, and no less important for God's chosen people than for any other tribe. After all, it's not as if being chosen makes you immune from dark periods of history. It doesn't. And the consequences can be devastating, as Psalm 78 recounts. Time and again God performed wonders in the desert; time and again Israel refused to trust. God delivered his people in exodus; the people made idols in the land. But for the fact that God's anger is on a slow burner, Israel's story would have ended right there. As the teacher points out, however, toward the end of his lengthy lesson, not only did Israel's story not end, it was about to enter its golden era. No sooner had God dismantled Shiloh, he built a sanctuary. And no sooner had he wiped out a generation, he found what he had long been searching for: a quiet shepherd to tend to his flock.

Prayer: *What a strange and tortured history we come from, Lord. Thank you that you didn't give up on us but brought us instead into your dreamtime. In Jesus name. Amen.*

Psalm 79
Community Lament

¹⁰ Why should the nations say,
  "Where is their God?"
Before our eyes, make known among the nations
  that you avenge the outpoured blood of your servants.
¹¹ May the groans of the prisoners come before you;
  with your strong arm preserve those condemned to die.
¹² Pay back into the laps of our neighbors seven times
  the contempt they have hurled at you, Lord.

JUST WHEN YOU THINK it is safe to get back in the water, swim a bit in the sweet sentiments of faith, here is another psalm that contains a real bite. And as much as we might try to justify it as righteous anger, it's hard to escape the feeling that this is all about raw vengeance. Set in contrast to the command of Jesus that we forgive our brother not just seven times but seventy times seven, the prayer at the end of the psalm for sevenfold pay-back sounds very shrill indeed. It sounds positively barbaric. But then again, what do we expect? This is no small drama. This is the loss of the temple. This is having the heart ripped out of the core of your community. This is separation from everything you hold to be true. To not cry vengeance on those who have done this is to contort one's emotions into an impossible bind. One hopes that eventually the rawness will subside. One hopes that eventually forgiveness will be offered, even to our enemies. But Psalm 79 sneaks into the Psalter to warn us that sometimes it can be offered too quickly. After all, one can only forgive when one has truly cried.

Prayer: *What a relief, Lord, that I can bring my deepest cries to you and know that, for all their rawness, you hear me. Amen.*

Psalm 80

Community Lament

¹² Why have you broken down its walls
   so that all who pass by pick its grapes?
¹³ Boars from the forest ravage it,
   and insects from the fields feed on it.
¹⁴ Return to us, God Almighty!
   Look down from heaven and see!
Watch over this vine,
   ¹⁵   the root your right hand has planted,
   the son you have raised up for yourself.

THE PSALMS CHOOSE THEIR images carefully. The righteous are like a tree, planted like streams of water; the wicked are like chaff blown in the wind, and so on. Psalm 80 begins with a familiar and comforting image of the Lord as a shepherd of Israel, leading his people like a flock. Later in the psalm, however, the image of God's people changes from a flock of sheep to that of a vine planted in the land. And a good job too that it's a vine. Had it been a rose, or a leaf—both national symbols—doubtless Israel would not have survived the ravages of judgment and persecution. She would not have endured the questions posed by the destruction of the temple. Being a vine, however—tough and tenacious—not only will Israel survive but also thrive in Jesus who said "I am the vine, you are the branches" (John 15:5).

It is good to pray this psalm. It holds on to the promise that God's mercy triumphs over his judgments. It vows, as only God's people can vow, that as God turns to us we will turn to him. And finally, it confirms to us the power of liturgy. "Lord, let your face shine upon us" is no token blessing but a guttural cry for salvation.

Prayer: *Lord, you can see how desperate things are. It's time for you to come down and save us. Amen.*

Psalm 81
Hymn with Prophetic Warning

[8] Hear me, my people, and I will warn you—
  if you would only listen to me, Israel!
[9] You shall have no foreign god among you;
  you shall not worship any god other than me.
[10] I am the LORD your God,
  who brought you up out of Egypt.
Open wide your mouth and I will fill it.

WORSHIP, BY DEFINITION, IS exuberant. How could it not be? We have so much to celebrate. But sometimes the combination of strings, percussion, singing, and happy clapping can get ahead of itself, to the point that the congregation can get carried along on a wave of emotion without ever really hearing the call of God. No chance of that here, however. No sooner does the band start up for the New Year festival than the prophet comes to the stage to warn the people that there can be no festivities without serious discipleship: no singing of songs without listening also to the voice of God. This is difficult to do, of course. There are so many other voices out there, demanding that we listen to them. Refusing to listen to God, however, is a perilous business, as the wilderness generation found out. It makes God mad that we should spurn his beneficence. And the worst thing about his judgment is not defeat in battle, as such, but being handed over to the stubbornness of our hearts. For all the autonomy it asserts, it is in fact the most miserable of states because it forfeits the riches of God.

Prayer: *O Lord, I would rather hear the harshness of your voice than nothing at all. Please, whatever happens, do not hand me over to the hardness of my heart. Amen.*

Psalm 82
Hymn with Prophetic Warning

[1] God presides in the great assembly;
   he renders judgment among the "gods":
[2] "How long will you defend the unjust
   and show partiality to the wicked?
[3] Defend the weak and the fatherless;
   uphold the cause of the poor and the oppressed.
[4] Rescue the weak and the needy;
   deliver them from the hand of the wicked."

SINCE JUSTICE AND RIGHTEOUSNESS are the foundation of God's world, then it stands to reason that the world seems a very fragile place indeed when injustice is allowed to reign. In fact, you could argue from this psalm that the perversion of justice is really the first step toward the apocalypse. The only thing that prevents it is God's intervention. In the divine council he calls the gods of the earth to account. He conducts an inquiry to see which of the gods may in fact qualify as gods, knowing already the heavy sentence he is about to carry out. After all, a society is only as good as the way it treats its most vulnerable people—the weak, the widow, the orphan and the destitute. Gods can only really be gods if they have a bias to the poor. The psalm ends with a cry for God to do on the earth what he has done in heaven, and bring justice to the world.

It's no wonder the early Christians found it easy to confess Jesus as God. In bringing good news to the poor Jesus does the things that God does, and lays claim to divinity in ways more powerful than any theological tract.

Prayer: *Lord, I am so happy that you have come out on top in the heavenly courtroom. Now make it happen here on earth. Your kingdom come, your will be done, on earth as it is in heaven. Amen.*

Psalm 83

Community Lament

¹³ Make them like tumbleweed, my God,
   like chaff before the wind.
¹⁴ As fire consumes the forest
   or a flame sets the mountains ablaze,
¹⁵ so pursue them with your tempest
   and terrify them with your storm.
¹⁶ Cover their faces with shame, LORD,
   so that they will seek your name.

WHATEVER ELSE THIS LAST of Asaph's psalms represents in terms of a prayer for justice, the outstanding thing about Psalm 83 is that it is honest and specific—probably one of the reasons why we don't hear it prayed much in church, where prayer can be anything but honest and specific. Indeed, our prayers can be so surface and general that it is a wonder they elicit any response at all. By comparison, the honesty in Psalm 83 goes deep. It is honest enough to pray what we all secretly long for but dare not admit, which is not only the defeat of our enemies but also their shaming. To be fair, there is a hint somewhere in this that maybe defeat will bring about a turning to God among the nations. But whatever hint there might be of a universal vision, it is more than obscured by the delight of imagining our enemies bowing the knee just before they perish. In other words, it is not a pleasant prayer. But then again, who said prayer has to be pleasant? We've had enough of these imprecations to realize that prayer more often than not is lodging our anger. And we do so in the confidence that God is not deaf, nor will he be mute forever.

Prayer: *Lord, I know I should have more pious thoughts than these, but just now this is what I am feeling. Thank you for giving me these words with which to pray my vengeance to you. Amen.*

Psalm 84

Zion Psalm

¹ How lovely is your dwelling place,
  Lord Almighty!
² My soul yearns, even faints,
  for the courts of the Lord;
my heart and my flesh cry out
  for the living God.

I TEND TO AGREE with American writer Kathleen Norris that when it comes to the Psalms only the King James will do. There is something about its rhythm and cadence which is unsurpassed. That's not to say, however, that the King James always gets it right. The opening of Psalm 84 is a case in point. To declare in true English reserve "O LORD how amiable are your courts" just doesn't get anywhere near what in the Hebrew is an almost erotic longing for the presence of God. And why not? This is a psalm of the sons of Korah—passionate poets if ever there were. The intensity of thought continues as the psalmist envies the little birds that lodge in the sacred walls while he is miles away in exile. Such is the strength of his desire, he would gladly trade a lifetime of opulence just for one day as a steward in the house of God.

It is good for us to pray this psalm: good for us to feel the frustration, the unrequitedness even, of a pilgrim's progress; and good, finally, to know that along the way, sometimes in the most unpromising terrain, God provides what we need to make it to the end.

Prayer: *O Lord of hosts, there is nowhere more delightful than being in your presence. Listen to my longing and satisfy my desire. Amen.*

Psalm 85

Community Lament

⁴ Restore us again, God our Savior,
  and put away your displeasure toward us.
⁵ Will you be angry with us forever?
  Will you prolong your anger through all generations?
⁶ Will you not revive us again,
  that your people may rejoice in you?
⁷ Show us your unfailing love, LORD,
  and grant us your salvation.

WHO KNOWS FULLY WHAT the setting is for this psalm. Babylonian exile seems the most likely. But then again, the verbs are so fluid that it could be an entirely different period of Israel's history. Either way, its enduring power lies not in its historical specifics but in its spiritual dynamics: namely, the cry, whoever we are, and whatever period we live in, for God to revive us. After all, nothing suffers so much from time as religion. We may start out in the first flush of enthusiasm but it's not long and we are sitting in the pew outwardly present but inwardly dead. And so we pray this prayer so that we might rejoice once again. As we pray this prayer to the end, however, hearing also the voice of the prophet to us, we realize we are being caught up in a plea not simply for personal revival but cosmic restoration. We find ourselves praying, in fact, for nothing less than God's kingdom to come, on earth as it is in heaven. And if as a result of praying this psalm we are left breathless, that is because the glory that awaits us is a kiss.

Prayer: *Lord, you call us to be joyful, but how can we be joyful unless you yourself revive us. Come quickly and save us. Revive the revival. Amen.*

Psalm 86
Individual Lament

[11] Teach me your way, LORD,
   that I may rely on your faithfulness;
give me an undivided heart,
   that I may fear your name.
[12] I will praise you, Lord my God, with all my heart;
   I will glorify your name forever.
[13] For great is your love toward me;
   you have delivered me from the depths,
   from the realm of the dead.

PRAYING THE PSALMS IN sequence, which is how they are meant to be prayed, one will have encountered almost every line of Psalm 86 elsewhere. In fact, it feels like a litany of all previous petitions placed into one psalm, interspersed with a heavy emphasis on the "you" of God's faithfulness rather than the "I" of personal lament. Among the many petitions that we are drawn into when we pray this psalm, there is one petition that stands out, gathering all the others together, which is the prayer for an undivided heart: a single petition for a single heart; one outstanding prayer for God to make our heart one.

Our hearts of course can be anything but single. Not only can our heart feel divided, it can feel fragmented—broken even. It seems that we are a bundle of contradictions, and at the mercy of jumbled desires. Coming into line would be something of a miracle. But then maybe this is what prayer is. Just by our saying the words, God gifts us with the grace of singularity, so that we might fear his name. Kierkegaard provides the best commentary on this: "purity of heart is to will one thing."

Prayer: *Lord, make my eye single so that my whole body will be full of light. Amen.*

Psalm 87

Zion Psalm

⁵ Indeed, of Zion it will be said,
  "This one and that one were born in her,
  and the Most High himself will establish her."
⁶ The LORD will write in the register of the peoples:
  "This one was born in Zion."
⁷ As they make music they will sing,
  "All my fountains are in you."

ROOTS ARE INCREDIBLY IMPORTANT. To know where we have come from is central to the formation of an identity. The fact that I was born in a particular place, in a particular country, at a particular time is not incidental to a life of faith but integral to it. Deeper than our natural roots, however, according to this short but universal psalm, are the wells of salvation from which we have sprung. And at this point, all eyes are on Jerusalem. Here, in the cradle of living faith, in the city where eventually Jesus himself will offer his life, we find our real identity, which goes way beyond our natural conception and back into the annals of grace. In fact, in praying this psalm, it's as if we are being encouraged to put aside our family tree, our regional accents, and our national pride, and lay hold of a spiritual identity that is as glorious as it is eternal.

Prayer: *Lord, I want to be one of those who dances for joy because they know who they are and whom they have believed. Hear my prayer. Amen.*

Psalm 88
Individual Lament

¹⁵ From my youth I have suffered and been close to death;
  I have borne your terrors and am in despair.
¹⁶ Your wrath has swept over me;
  your terrors have destroyed me.
¹⁷ All day long they surround me like a flood;
  they have completely engulfed me.
¹⁸ You have taken from me friend and neighbor—
  darkness is my closest friend.

THERE IS SOME DEBATE as to the correct translation of the last line of Psalm 88. It is difficult to decide whether it is "darkness is my only friend," or more the idea that since his friends have withdrawn themselves from him, they are "nothing but darkness to him." Whichever translation we opt for, neither avoids the unique and disturbing feature of this psalm of lament: namely, that there is no resolution. Whereas other laments turn on the pivot of praise, of answered prayer, or a priest's assurance, here there is no such comforting end. All we have is an unrelenting dark night of the soul. It is important, however, that this prayer made the collection—even if it does sound more like a Leonard Cohen song than a psalm—because sometimes this is exactly how it feels: God seems to have abandoned us. No matter how much we cry out, there is no answer. No amount of arm-twisting gets a response. And to have at least one psalm that acknowledges this, that takes seriously the prolonged absence of God, reminds us, however painful, that prayer is not formulaic, less so predictable, but a lively exchange with the God who is free. This is small comfort, I know, for the one who feels abandoned, except that the psalm itself affirms that persistent prayer, even when there is no sign of an answer, is the supreme act of faith.

Prayer: *Some days, Lord, this darkness is exactly what I feel. Thank you that you understand and allow me to bring even this to you. Amen.*

Psalm 89

Royal

³⁸ But you have rejected, you have spurned,
   you have been very angry with your anointed one.
³⁹ You have renounced the covenant with your servant
   and have defiled his crown in the dust.
⁴⁰ You have broken through all his walls
   and reduced his strongholds to ruins.
⁴¹ All who pass by have plundered him;
   he has become the scorn of his neighbors.

HAVING JUST MADE THE statement that Psalm 88 is unique among the laments for not having a resolution, apart for the final doxology the same could be said of Psalm 89. And in any case, the doxology is probably there to bring Book III to a close, rather than bring Psalm 89 to a resolution. What is different about Psalm 89, however, in contrast to the previous psalm, is that the questioning of God's faithfulness comes off the back of a celebration of God's faithfulness. In fact, it could be described as a psalm of two halves: the first half extravagant in praise of God's covenant with David, Israel's golden king; the second half extreme in protest for the covenant with David, Israel's plundered crown. In some ways the protest is all the more accusatory precisely because the praise was so affirmative—at times it sounds like blasphemy. God made a covenant with David, which he seems to have reneged on. In true Job fashion, everything now seems futile.

Wouldn't it have been lovely had Psalm 89 ended at v. 37? Wouldn't it be wonderful to inhabit a world of pure festal joy? But we don't. Ours is a broken Hallelujah. But just as faithfulness in this psalm is the backdrop to brokenness, maybe brokenness can be a prelude to faithfulness. Certainly that is how Christians understand the coming of Jesus, the Son of David.

Prayer: *Hosanna, Lord save us. Blessed is he who comes in the name of the Lord. Amen.*

Book IV

Psalm 90

Community Lament

³ You turn people back to dust,
  saying, "Return to dust, you mortals."
⁴ A thousand years in your sight
  are like a day that has just gone by,
  or like a watch in the night.
⁵ Yet you sweep people away in the sleep of death—
  they are like the new grass of the morning:
⁶ In the morning it springs up new,
  but by evening it is dry and withered.

TIME IS A STRANGE commodity. It has an elasticity about it. When you are young it seems that life spreads out in front of you like an eternity, but soon enough you begin to realize that we are ephemeral—that the only eternity is in God. We are no more substantial than the morning grass that springs up yet by evening time is dry and withered. Rather than get depressed by this, however, or overly dismayed by the hot breath of God's fury, the psalmist derives wisdom from this numbering of days. To own one's mortality is in fact the first step of grace because it causes us to reach out to God in prayer. And God is the master of time. It's not so much that he adds years to your life; rather, that he changes the quality of them so that what feels so fleeting can become fulfilling. As God satisfies us each new morning with his love, so our lives take on new meaning. Days become years in a life that, for all its brevity, is surprisingly substantial because it is rooted in the everlasting God.

Prayer: *Teach me indeed, dear Lord, to number my days aright, so that I will live grateful for each new morning. Amen.*

Psalm 91

Trust Psalm

¹ Whoever dwells in the shelter of the Most High
    will rest in the shadow of the Almighty.
² I will say of the LORD, "He is my refuge and my fortress,
    my God, in whom I trust."

THE WORLD IS A dangerous place. On the surface of it Psalm 91 seems to promise us immunity from it. And yet we all know this is not the case. We all know people who have been struck by disaster. So what's it all about? And why did the devil quote Psalm 91 to Jesus in the wilderness? Well, for a start, this is not a theological treatise on suffering, nor the final word on evil, but a pastoral encouragement. I've even heard it described as an amulet that we pray out loud whenever we doubt the faithfulness of God. Try it. Given the power of the opening lines, almost immediately you find yourself in the warmth of a safe shelter, under what Hopkins calls "the mothering wing" of God. And no, it's not that we are whisked away from the action. This psalm is full of drama. But there in the shadow of the Almighty we can be sure of God's protecting love. I think this is why Jesus resisted the temptation to jump from the temple. Not only did he not want to put God to the test, he already knew that whatever happened to him, and however dark things would become, God's angels would strengthen him. Gethsemane proved him right.

Prayer: *Lord, when I am frightened, I am not going to run away, nor am I going to take matters into my own hands. I am simply going to place myself under the shadow of your wings. Amen.*

Psalm 92
Individual Psalm of Thanksgiving

¹² The righteous will flourish like a palm tree,
   they will grow like a cedar of Lebanon;
¹³ planted in the house of the LORD,
   they will flourish in the courts of our God.
¹⁴ They will still bear fruit in old age,
   they will stay fresh and green,
¹⁵ proclaiming, "The LORD is upright;
   he is my Rock, and there is no wickedness in him."

IT CAN BE VERY discouraging living a life of faith. We appear to live in a world in which crime pays while good old fashioned values are ridiculed. Psalm 92 attests to a deeper design, however (which only fools can't see), where these things are turned on their head. Once you have your eyes open to God, you begin to see that for all the impressiveness of short-term fame, evil has a very tenuous existence indeed. Righteousness, on the other hand, is as solid as a tree. In fact, "long obedience in the same direction" has a certain freshness about it. It has a vigor that seems to grow stronger the older you get, whereas evil tires easily.

It is not insignificant that this psalm is attributed to the Sabbath day. After all, where else do we lay hold of these deeper truths except in the merry-making of Sabbath-day worship? In the simple rhythm of morning and evening praise we become attuned to God's world which then makes sense of our world. As we leave the precincts of worship we see everything through the lens of exuberant faith.

Prayer: *O God Most High, it is indeed good to set this day before you: to declare your love in the morning and your faithfulness at night. Amen.*

Psalm 93

Enthronement

¹ The LORD reigns, he is robed in majesty;
    the LORD is robed in majesty and armed with strength;
    indeed, the world is established, firm and secure.
² Your throne was established long ago;
    you are from all eternity.

ACCORDING TO GENESIS, GOD formed the world out of chaos. There have been times, however, and may be more times yet, when it seems to want to return back to chaos. Indeed, when the temple was destroyed and the people went into exile—so very much the theme of Book III of the Psalter—it was so catastrophic that it felt like the end of the world. Psalm 93, however, stands as a bulwark against the tide. This short but powerful psalm, which some think might be the very heart of the Psalter, reminds this people who live precariously on the eastern edge of the Mediterranean that no matter how mighty is the thunder of the great waters, no matter how much the seas are lifted up, the Lord is mightier still. And it's not that in saying this psalm somehow we are putting God on the throne. The truth of the matter is that God has always been reigning, and always will. As the psalmist puts it, he is robed in majesty and strength. But maybe by praying it, both privately and corporately, we assure our hearts once again, when chaos comes crashing in like waves, that the world is firmly established, it cannot be moved. Christians do this of course every Easter. In the midst of uncertainty, and sometimes despite all the evidence, we proclaim "Christ the Lord is risen today."

Prayer: *Eternal Father, I am so strengthened by the knowledge that at the center of all things is a throne, your throne. Amen.*

Psalm 94

Individual Lament

⁸ Take notice, you senseless ones among the people;
  you fools, when will you become wise?
⁹ Does he who fashioned the ear not hear?
  Does he who formed the eye not see?
¹⁰ Does he who disciplines nations not punish?
  Does he who teaches mankind lack knowledge?
¹¹ The LORD knows all human plans;
  he knows that they are futile.

IN A SOCIETY THAT has become increasingly decadent, dismissive of the poor and needy, and derisory of God's ability to act, Psalm 94 is a confident assertion that God will have the final word. After all, God sees everything. The idea that human beings are autonomous is an illusion. Where justice is not maintained, God will side with the poor. Indeed, he will bring such consolations to the suffering that instead of feeling victimized they will know a kind of holy cheer. Which makes one wonder why this psalm is not more popular, or well-known. Maybe it's because we feel a little uncomfortable with the anger expressed here, or not entirely sure how happiness and chastisement sit together. But the thing about the Psalms is that as long as we say them to God we can literally say everything we feel. There is nothing that we cannot lay at God's door, in the confidence that he hears us. And who knows? Maybe honesty is what happiness is all about.

Prayer: *Lord, help me not to be intimidated by the rich and the powerful. Teach me how to live close to your unfailing love. Amen.*

Psalm 95

Enthronement

Today, if only you would hear his voice,
⁸ "Do not harden your hearts as you did at Meribah,
   as you did that day at Massah in the wilderness,
⁹ where your ancestors tested me;
   they tried me, though they had seen what I did.
¹⁰ For forty years I was angry with that generation;
   I said, 'They are a people whose hearts go astray,
   and they have not known my ways.'
¹¹ So I declared on oath in my anger,
   'They shall never enter my rest.'"

ALL GENUINE WORSHIP HAS an urgency about it. Yes, it should be uplifting, and yes it should be affirming. Who wants worship that does not stir the emotions and makes us feel good? The first half of this psalm does both. But true worship also strikes a note of immediacy. Call it revivalism if you want, but at some point or other someone needs to stand up and proclaim "today if you hear his voice, do not harden your heart," otherwise we could end up simply pussy-footing around the precincts of faith. Worse still, we could end up like the wilderness generation, wandering aimlessly around the desert, and never actually experiencing God's best. Which all goes to say that worship is a serious business (Heb 3:7–13). We come not to be entertained but to keep on keeping on in the way of faith. It is this present-tense openness to the voice of God that is the heart of worship and the hallmark of holiness.

Prayer: *Lord, I do not want to miss out on your best because of cynicism, unbelief, or even procrastination. Help me to keep my heart ever responsive to your living word. Begin in me today. Amen*

Psalm 96
Enthronement

⁷ Ascribe to the Lord, all you families of nations,
   ascribe to the Lord glory and strength.
⁸ Ascribe to the Lord the glory due his name;
   bring an offering and come into his courts.
⁹ Worship the Lord in the splendor of his holiness;
   tremble before him, all the earth.
¹⁰ Say among the nations, "The Lord reigns."
   The world is firmly established, it cannot be moved;
   he will judge the peoples with equity.

THERE IS A WONDERFUL universality in this psalm. You only have to pray it to feel it. Not just Israel, but all the peoples of the earth are enjoined to celebrate God's kingship. Such is the scope of God's reign that his royal arrival is welcomed not only by the peoples of the earth but the whole of the creation: roaring seas, singing trees, and jubilant fields. It is a riot of color and noise. It is not just the breadth and the depth of things, however, that strikes the reader of this psalm, but the height as well: the ascriptions to God of something the world so desperately lacks, which is glory. In fact, it would be hard to come away from this psalm without feeling sanctified by sheer wonder at the beauty of the Lord. In praying it, we are treading on "heaven's embroidered cloths" (Yeats), which is possibly why the psalmist insists that this is a new song. The newness is surely not the content. Most of these lines we have heard before. The newness is in the world that is opened up to us, now that we have entered his courts.

Prayer: *O God, above and beyond anything else we can pray for, give us glory. Glory in the church and in Christ Jesus. Amen.*

Psalm 97
Enthronement

² Clouds and thick darkness surround him;
   righteousness and justice are the foundation of his throne.
³ Fire goes before him
   and consumes his foes on every side.
⁴ His lightning lights up the world;
   the earth sees and trembles.
⁵ The mountains melt like wax before the LORD,
   before the Lord of all the earth.
⁶ The heavens proclaim his righteousness,
   and all peoples see his glory.

IN THIS SEQUENCE OF psalms which celebrate God's kingly reign, we move from the God who rules the waves, in Psalm 96, to the God of thunder and lightning, here in Psalm 97. It is a journey that takes us even deeper into mystery. Clouds and thick darkness surround him. But it is also a journey that establishes things because we realize that his throne is founded on the solid rock of righteousness and justice. As a result, his praise reaches the distant coastlands, for this is none other than the God of Sinai. So substantial is his rule—so real his presence—that solid mountains melt to wax. And such gods as exist are nothing but idols in comparison. To borrow a thought from Annie Dillard, it's a wonder that the ushers don't issue us with crash helmets as we come to worship such a God. The fact that the writer to the Hebrews teaches us that the fear of Sinai had been replaced by the joy of Zion—the joy of Jesus in fact—should not lessen our awe but increase it (Heb 13:29). In the end, grace is not the denial of judgment but the triumphing over it.

Prayer: *O Lord, I will rejoice in you for you have delivered me from the dull dreariness of idolatrous living. Amen.*

Psalm 98
Enthronement

⁷ Let the sea resound, and everything in it,
   the world, and all who live in it.
⁸ Let the rivers clap their hands,
   let the mountains sing together for joy;
⁹ let them sing before the LORD,
   for he comes to judge the earth.
He will judge the world in righteousness
   and the peoples with equity.

IT IS NOT ALWAYS the case that you find liveliness as well as theological depth in the sanctuary. Sometimes the worship is full of passion but no content; or full of content but no passion. Psalm 98, which continues the cycle of kingship psalms, wonderfully combines both. It is exuberant in praise, yet mindful always of the reasons why. The key word is "for": "Sing to the LORD a new song, *for* he has done marvellous things." In fact the more the Psalm recounts the great salvation of God, the more exuberant the worship. To the human orchestra of trumpet, horns, and lyre are added the percussive claps of rivers and the chorus sound of mountains. All creation joins together in a panoply of praise. And why not? After a long exile, God has remembered his love and faithfulness to Israel. He has triumphed over the forces of chaos. He has made known his victory, says the psalmist, to the ends of the earth. If that doesn't raise a shout, what will? This is pure gospel.

Prayer: *I thank you, Lord, that I wake to a world of wonder—to a world you have redeemed. Help me to find my singing voice so that I can praise you with unashamed abandon. Amen.*

Psalm 99

Enthronement

[4] The King is mighty, he loves justice—
  you have established equity;
in Jacob you have done
  what is just and right.
[5] Exalt the LORD our God
  and worship at his footstool;
  he is holy.

HOLY IS A WORD that is used a great deal in liturgy. In this psalm it occurs three times as a refrain: "Holy is he." The overall effect, however, is not to create distance, as we might expect from the word holy, but to nurture hope. For this is a God who is deeply involved with his world, protecting the powerless from oppression by the powerful, and wanting life to flourish under his rule. To tremble before this King is not to be frightened of him but to follow him by seeking to live with integrity, all the while conscious that he is also a forgiving God, and one who answers when we pray. Moses and Aaron knew that. So did Samuel. They knew that for all the demands of the covenant it also meant relationship—the freedom to bring literally anything before God. For a people who were in exile, devoid of their temple, this was good news indeed. Psalm 99 reminds them that they have a history with God that predates the monarchy. And to us who struggle through our own wilderness, wondering how we will survive, Psalm 99 reminds us that God's greatness transcends everything.

Prayer: *O Lord my God, as I bow down before your holy throne, I thank you that I feel nothing but warmth and invitation. Through Jesus Christ, Amen.*

Psalm 100
General Hymn

⁴ Enter his gates with thanksgiving
　　and his courts with praise;
　　　give thanks to him and praise his name.
⁵ For the LORD is good and his love endures forever;
　　his faithfulness continues through all generations.

GIVEN THE RELATIVELY STATIC nature of congregational worship in the West, with so much of our time seated in rows, it is instructive to note the active and somewhat noisy nature of the Psalms, Psalm 100 being one of the best and most familiar examples. Through seven imperatives—make a joyful noise, worship, come, know, enter, give thanks, and bless—we are called to pilgrimage. As we respond, we find ourselves moving with anticipation from the outskirts, through the gates, and into the courts of the temple. On account of a royal summons, as opposed to a personal quest, it is in fact a journey from the profane to the sacred. And even if we cannot actually make that physical journey, because of course there is now no literal temple (and Jesus himself is now the dwelling place of God), maybe to simply pray it is enough to excite the imagination and lead us to the place where we too can worship the Lord with gladness. This is what God's people do. In gratitude, they flock together to praise him for his steadfast love and mercy.

Prayer: *Dear Lord, I am just astonished that I find myself among your people, thanking and praising you for your great love. I never knew life could be this good. Amen.*

Psalm 101
Royal

[1] I will sing of your love and justice;
   to you, LORD, I will sing praise.
[2] I will be careful to lead a blameless life—
   when will you come to me?
I will conduct the affairs of my house
   with a blameless heart.
[3] I will not look with approval
   on anything that is vile.

ONE HAS TO ADMIRE the resolve of the psalmist to live a blameless life: to do what is right and eschew what is evil. To pray this psalm is to give voice to a rare kind of moral steeliness, which in a culture that has become ethically flabby is no small thing. Of course, we don't want to be praying psalms of this sort all the time—that way lies self-righteousness. But to have them appear once in a while adds ballast to our fragile will, and keeps us ever vigilant of the deceitfulness of the heart—both our own and others. Before embarking on this psalm, however, we should note that for all the well-spoken professions of faithfulness that these eight verses contain, and for all his disdain for slander and deceit, the psalmist knows as well as anyone that unless the Lord comes to him and graces him with his presence, all his earnestness will be for nothing. In other words, we need to remember that Psalm 101 is a prayer and not a response to an altar call. And the prayer is as urgent as it is familiar: your kingdom come, your will be done.

Prayer: *Dear Lord, in a world that has become ever more decadent, help me to maintain a moral vision. Amen.*

Psalm 102

Individual Lament

¹² But you, LORD, sit enthroned forever;
  your renown endures through all generations.
¹³ You will arise and have compassion on Zion,
  for it is time to show favor to her;
  the appointed time has come.
¹⁴ For her stones are dear to your servants;
  her very dust moves them to pity.

UNTYPICALLY, THE HEADING TO this psalm could actually be the first line of the prayer. It seems to fit the psalm itself, rather than just acting as an editorial. Either way, what follows are some of the most startling images of personal affliction that one could imagine: the charred remains of a smouldering hearth; withered grass; a night owl among the ruins. As the psalmist tosses and turns in bed, unable to sleep, he imagines himself like the lonely bird on the roof whose scratchings he can hear. Desolation is everywhere.

Yet for all the groaning inside, for all the mocking of his enemies, for all the sense of the fragility of life, the psalmist can still raise a "But you" kind of prayer (v. 12). In the evening of his life, with the shadows lengthening on the sundial, he is able, nevertheless, to confess a faith in the King who reigns forever. Long after even the heavens and the earth wear out, he knows that God will endure, for God's years never end. Above all, he knows that this God will not despise the prayers of the destitute, be it his own or that of the nation as a whole, whose plight, bizarrely, he identifies with. And the reason he believes this is because he knows that beyond judgment lies grace.

Prayer: *Lord, just when I feel abandoned, I remember that it is my frailty that arouses your compassion. Amen.*

Psalm 103

General Hymn

¹ Praise the LORD, my soul;
   all my inmost being, praise his holy name.
² Praise the LORD, my soul,
   and forget not all his benefits—
³ who forgives all your sins
   and heals all your diseases,
⁴ who redeems your life from the pit
   and crowns you with love and compassion,
⁵ who satisfies your desires with good things
   so that your youth is renewed like the eagle's.

THIS IS SUCH A well-known psalm that it is easy to overlook the fact that it has such an unusual beginning. The opening self-exhortation—Praise the Lord, my soul—is as striking as the litany of verbs that follow. In a rising crescendo we come to bless the Lord, who not just forgives, but heals; not just heals, but redeems; not just redeems, but crowns; not just crowns, but satisfies; not just satisfies, but renews. The whole of the psalm in fact is a tonic to faith. Here we are thinking that God is just waiting to vent his spleen on us, only to be told that things are better than we could have possibly imagined. His anger, we discover, is actually on a safety lock, whereas his mercy is on a hair trigger. Furthermore, the vertical axis of God's great love for those who fear him is wonderfully matched by the horizontal distance that God places between us and our sins. The vast distance between east and west, as well as the fatherly compassion that God has upon our fragile frame, is simply another way of saying *gospel*.

Prayer: *Loving Lord, you tend and spare us, well our feeble frame you know. In your hands you gently bear us, rescue us from all our foes. Praise you, Hallelujah.*

Psalm 104
Creation

¹³ He waters the mountains from his upper chambers;
the land is satisfied by the fruit of his work.
¹⁴ He makes grass grow for the cattle,
and plants for people to cultivate—
bringing forth food from the earth:
¹⁵ wine that gladdens human hearts,
oil to make their faces shine,
and bread that sustains their hearts

THERE ARE NO NATURE poems in the Psalms; only psalms in praise of the Creator. Long before any concepts of ecosystems, the psalmist delights in the right-ordering of everything—mountains and valleys; springs and streams; sun and moon; animals and people. But rather than attribute this to the impersonal forces of nature he sees them as the providence of God. It is this holy intricacy of the created world, rather than any speculative enquiry into notions of God's eternity, that forms the basis of our worship here—the opening line of Hopkins' best-known poem being as good a commentary as we might find on this matter: "The world is charged with the grandeur of God." And precisely because everything is charged with God's grandeur, then we need not be anxious about the future. As naive as it sounds, such is the generative power of God, the renewing breath of his Spirit, that even death can come to life. Furthermore, we should not be surprised that the triad of elemental gifts singled out in the psalm—wine, oil, and bread—feature prominently in the sacramental life of the church. To use the words of the eucharistic liturgy, they are celebrated as "symbols of our world, and signs of his transforming love."

Prayer: *Dear Lord, I just love the fact that your salvation takes place in the theatre of our created world and not in some cul-de-sac of religious piety. Help us to be expansive in our praise. Amen.*

Psalm 105

General Hymn

¹⁶ He called down famine on the land
   and destroyed all their supplies of food;
¹⁷ and he sent a man before them—
   Joseph, sold as a slave.
¹⁸ They bruised his feet with shackles,
   his neck was put in irons,
¹⁹ till what he foretold came to pass,
   till the word of the LORD proved him true.

CHRONOLOGICAL SEQUENCES ARE NOT generally thought of as the most thrilling way to teach history, unless of course your history is littered with astonishing acts of divine grace, in which case you have no choice other than to simply tell it as it is. Hence the length of Psalm 105. Everything needs to be put in, from the patriarchs to the exodus, all the way to the borders of the promised land. In fact, it is the promise of land that forms the backbone of the psalm, not in a colonial sense—although it has been used that way (1 Chr 16:8–22)—but in the sense of giving assurance to a beleaguered people that their God is the Lord of history and the deliverer of Israel. Sometimes, of course, God's ways are difficult to discern. The episode with Joseph for example is a case of inscrutability if ever there was. In what way can God be said to be at work when Joseph is sold into slavery by his brothers? The end of the story, however, reveals that even the most calamitous suffering can be the prelude to unbelievable providence. If that is not thrilling, I don't know what is.

Prayer: *I thank you, Lord, that you go before us, working all things together for the good of those who love you. Amen.*

Psalm 106

Community Lament

⁴³ Many times he delivered them,
    but they were bent on rebellion
    and they wasted away in their sin.
⁴⁴ Yet he took note of their distress
    when he heard their cry;
⁴⁵ for their sake he remembered his covenant
    and out of his great love he relented.
⁴⁶ He caused all who held them captive
    to show them mercy.

IF PSALM 105 IS the history of Israel which celebrates God's astonishing acts, Psalm 106 is the same history with all the awkward bits left in. Despite its promising opening, it quickly becomes a confession of Israel's rebelliousness. As a matter of fact, it is a history of Israel's forgetfulness. But since everything hinges on God's people remembering his great salvation, then forgetfulness soon leads to rebelliousness—on a grand scale. You name it, Israel was guilty of it: mutiny, idolatry, unbelief, cynicism, and syncretism. It reads like one of those horrible histories. Yes, there are moments of reprieve, Phineas being one of the few to come out of the psalm with distinction. But overall Israel's history is a litany of failure. Fortunately, however, the people's forgetting is more than matched by God's remembering. And for the psalmist, remembering means gathering from all the nations of the earth so that we may glory in his praise. Thus concludes Book IV of the Psalms; or is it chapter 1 of the gospel?

Prayer: *It is amazing, Lord, how fickle we are. It's a wonder you don't wash your hands of us. Thank you that you don't, and give us instead what we don't deserve. Amazing grace. Amen.*

Book V

Psalm 107
Community Psalm of Thanksgiving

⁴ Some wandered in desert wastelands,
    finding no way to a city where they could settle.
⁵ They were hungry and thirsty,
    and their lives ebbed away.
⁶ Then they cried out to the LORD in their trouble,
    and he delivered them from their distress.
⁷ He led them by a straight way
    to a city where they could settle.

SOMETIMES IT IS ASTONISHING how quickly God answers our prayers. Here in Psalm 107 it's almost as if God delivers his people before they have even asked him. The gap between the cry going up to God and the Lord bringing them out of their distress is practically non-existent. Even so, it is important that we pray. Whether we find ourselves in a desert place, in a dark dungeon, on the verge of dying, or tossed about at sea, our cries to God are an acknowledgement to ourselves that we are not self-sufficient but utterly dependant on the steadfast love of God to see us through.

Praying such prayers is not easy in a culture that prizes self-made men and women, but absolutely central to what it means to live for God. After all, "He has the whole world in his hands." Not only can he turn rivers into deserts but also deserts into rivers. A wise person will not ignore this, nor pretend that they can wield similar power, but will instead live prayerfully in the knowledge that whatever distress we find ourselves in, God is able to rescue us. Call it weakness if you want. In the Psalms they call it thanksgiving.

Prayer: *Lord, in my troubles, help me turn quickly to you rather than stupidly to myself. Amen.*

Psalm 108

Community Lament

⁷ God has spoken from his sanctuary:
  "In triumph I will parcel out Shechem
  and measure off the Valley of Sukkoth.
⁸ Gilead is mine, Manasseh is mine;
  Ephraim is my helmet,
  Judah is my scepter.
⁹ Moab is my washbasin,
  on Edom I toss my sandal;
  over Philistia I shout in triumph."

"WHEN MORNING GILDS THE skies," says the hymn writer, "my heart awakening cries, may Jesus Christ be praised." Wonderful opening lines. But as much as the dawn light is the time for us to wake up to a life of praise, there is a sense here in Psalm 108 that our singing actually has the power to awaken the dawn. In the dim half-light, as we preside over the turning of the world, we rouse it by our singing to a life of faith in God. In fact, early morning praise has the effect of making everything come alive. Hitherto familiar places—Shechem, Succoth, Gilead, Manasseh, Ephraim, Judah—take on the mantle of God's kingdom; whereas traditionally hostile places—Moab, Edom, Philistia—at last come under God's rule, never to threaten again. Through early morning prayer our eyes are now fully open to a world of wonder—to what George Herbert called "heaven in ordinary." Whole towns, cities, and nations are transformed by the glory of God, for what is salvation but sanctified geography?

Psalm 108 is, of course, a stitching together of Psalm 57:8–12 and Psalm 60:6–14. Why this should be so is not entirely clear, other than that the two portions are some of the most beautiful poetry in the whole of the Psalter—thus making Psalm 108 a doubly beautiful prayer.

Prayer: *I thank you, Lord, that I wake to a world of wonder—a world of your triumph. Amen.*

Psalm 109

Individual Lament

²⁶ Help me, LORD my God;
  save me according to your unfailing love.
²⁷ Let them know that it is your hand,
  that you, LORD, have done it.
²⁸ While they curse, may you bless;
  may those who attack me be put to shame,
  but may your servant rejoice.
²⁹ May my accusers be clothed with disgrace
  and wrapped in shame as in a cloak.

MICHAEL HENCHARD, THE MAIN protagonist of Thomas Hardy's *The Mayor of Casterbridge,* is drinking with the choir after practice one day when he sees his rival, Donald Farfrae, whom he hates. He later persuades the choir to sing Psalm 109. The choir master remarks of this psalm that, "Twasn't made for singing. We chose it once when the gypsy stole the parson's mare, thinking to please him, but parson were quite upset. Whatever Servant David were thinking about when he made a Psalm that nobody can sing without disgracing himself, I can't fathom." Anyone who has prayed this psalm will no doubt feel the same. It feels sub-Christian, dangerous even. Yet, for all its vengeance, we have to come to terms with the fact that Psalm 109, sometimes known as the Judas Psalm, is as much a part of the Psalter as Psalm 23. Short of ripping it out of the Bible, in a kind of Marcionite objection to the Old Testament, we are called upon to pray it. And good job too because feelings of vengeance are real. Not one of us is unfamiliar with personal injustice, and the desire to see the worst happen to those who have hurt us. We can deny it if we want. Many nice religious types do. But all that will happen is that the anger will go underground. But by voicing it to God, as here in Psalm 109, we take the ultimate step of faith by placing it in his hands.

Prayer: *It is true that I feel wounded, Lord. Thank you for giving me words to express it, even as you give me grace to endure it. Amen.*

Psalm 110

Royal

² The LORD will extend your mighty scepter from Zion, saying,
  "Rule in the midst of your enemies!"
³ Your troops will be willing
  on your day of battle.
Arrayed in holy splendor,
  your young men will come to you
  like dew from the morning's womb.

WHEN I COME TO this psalm, so many images start flashing in my mind, quite literally in fact, because the first image that presents itself is line upon line of young men and women, their armor glistening like the early morning dew as they await orders to march into battle. Then I see the battle commence, carnage ensue, and the enemy crushed by the sheer weight of God's splendor. Above all, however, I see the coming together of two things that are essential if the world is to be fully healed: kingship and priesthood. Like all imagery of course, there comes a point when it fixes on something or someone concrete. For the earliest Christians this had to be Jesus, for in him are combined the authority to rule and the power to forgive: a king forever in the order of Melchizedek. Indeed, Psalm 110 is the most often-quoted psalm in the New Testament, presumably because it states so beautifully the reign of Christ until he makes his enemies a footstool for his feet (1 Cor 15:25)—the last enemy being death itself. Meanwhile, however, while we go about the work of the kingdom, this psalm reminds us that urgency is not the same as hurriedness. Such is the poise of the poet's master that he is able to pause in the heat of battle to drink beside the brook.

Prayer: *Lord, may our young people be full of willingness to enter into the fray of the battle, but always with a sense that you are victorious. Amen.*

Psalm 111
Individual Hymn of Thanksgiving

² Great are the works of the LORD;
   they are pondered by all who delight in them.
³ Glorious and majestic are his deeds,
   and his righteousness endures forever.
⁴ He has caused his wonders to be remembered;
   the LORD is gracious and compassionate.
⁵ He provides food for those who fear him;
   he remembers his covenant forever.

IF WE THINK WORSHIP is the joyful exuberance of a happy person, we are wrong. Rather, it is the grateful response of the redeemed. But that is not to say it needs to be dour. Instead, we must see worship as bringing the whole of ourselves before the whole of God, as the opening line of Psalm 111 describes. As the psalm develops, guiding us by way of an acrostic through the A-Z of God's works, it elicits a response that can best be described as intelligence on fire: that is to say, a powerful coming together of the mind, the will, and the emotions in a triumphant *Hallelujah!* And to this salvation song the psalmist welds a classic wisdom saying at the end, reminding us that "the fear of the LORD is the beginning of wisdom." In other words, right living is not a matter of sitting down on your own with a manual one day and working out how to do life, but rather being captivated week after week by the awesomeness of God. When this happens, it will be pretty obvious how we ought to live.

Prayer: *O Lord, astonish me once again with the wonder of your great love so that I might live in right fear of your name. Amen.*

Psalm 112

Wisdom

⁶ Surely the righteous will never be shaken;
   they will be remembered forever.
⁷ They will have no fear of bad news;
   their hearts are steadfast, trusting in the LORD.
⁸ Their hearts are secure, they will have no fear;
   in the end they will look in triumph on their foes.
⁹ They have freely scattered their gifts to the poor,
   their righteousness endures forever;
   their horn will be lifted high in honor.

THOSE WHO DEPEND ON the stock market or public opinion or even their health will always find themselves living on the edge. These things are as variable as the wind. Those who trust in the Lord, however, will have no fear of bad news. Because they have put their roots deep into God's word they will remain firm, says the psalmist, no matter what. Whilst others are guarding what they have, the righteous will continue to give away, secure in the knowledge that God will sustain our desire to be "generous on every occasion" (2 Cor 9:10).

With Psalm 112 we are right back at the beginning of the Psalter. As much as it is a pair with Psalm 111, Psalm 112 is like Psalm 1 in what it promises, but with one important difference: that the wisdom of this psalm has been formed, like many psalms in these latter books, through the trial of exile. Which means that it is all the more robust. There is nothing like experience to strengthen faith.

Prayer: *Lord, keep me ever open-handed to the poor of the world and ever grateful for all you have given me. Amen.*

Psalm 113
General Hymn

⁷ He raises the poor from the dust
  and lifts the needy from the ash heap;
⁸ he seats them with princes,
  with the princes of his people.
⁹ He settles the childless woman in her home
  as a happy mother of children.

IT IS NO SURPRISE to anyone who knows anything about religion that deity might be regarded as high and lofty. After all, power and majesty go with the territory of being God. What would be scandalous however, and worthy of note, is a combination of power on high and compassion below: that is, the descent of this high and lofty God into the needfulness of the earth. But that is precisely what we have here in Psalm 113. A more literal translation of the middle verses brings out the contrast beautifully: God "makes God's self high in order to sit; makes God's self low in order to see" (Brueggemann). In fact, God makes himself so low that he dignifies the most hopeless souls, lifting them up to a seat of royalty and a house of joy. Students of the Bible will have heard this before in the story of Hannah. Those familiar with the Gospels will remember Mary. But it is Jesus himself who fully embodies this first of the so-called Hallelujah Psalms. As they said of Jesus' earliest followers: "they turned the world upside down" (Acts 17:16).

Prayer: *It is incredible to me, Lord, that you don't use your power to your own advantage, but instead stoop down in order to raise us up. I praise you. Amen.*

Psalm 114

General Hymn

⁵ Why was it, sea, that you fled?
  Why, Jordan, did you turn back?
⁶ Why, mountains, did you leap like rams,
  you hills, like lambs?
⁷ Tremble, earth, at the presence of the Lord,
  at the presence of the God of Jacob,
⁸ who turned the rock into a pool,
  the hard rock into springs of water.

SALVATION STORIES ARE VERY much the stuff of vanquishing enemies, holy sanctuaries, and kingdom realities. Sadly, however, in the hands of a poor liturgist, the coming together of those concepts can create the impression that religious faith operates in special sanctified spaces, separate and unrelated to the world as we know it. No such danger here. As the psalmist bears witness to the great exodus event, the wilderness years, and the crossing of the Jordan into Jericho, it turns out that the whole creation is in a whirl. Solid mountains are leaping like lambs; imperious rivers and seas flee in fear; unyielding rocks gush forth water. It seems the whole earth is trembling before the presence of the God of Jacob. That which began as the salvation of a particular people is in fact the redemption of all created things. As the hymn writer George Herbert puts it—and he knew a thing or two about liturgy—"Let all the earth, in every corner sing, my God and King."

Prayer: *Praise you, Lord, that yours is a redemption not from the world but of the world. Help me never to separate the power of your redemption from the wonder of your creation. Amen.*

Psalm 115

General Hymn

¹ Not to us, LORD, not to us
  but to your name be the glory,
  because of your love and faithfulness.
² Why do the nations say,
  "Where is their God?"
³ Our God is in heaven;
  he does whatever pleases him.
⁴ But their idols are silver and gold,
  made by human hands.

FANS OF SHAKESPEARE WILL find it hard to read the opening line of Psalm 115 without resorting to the victory song in Henry V: *"Non nobis, Domine, non nobis, sed nomini tuo da gloriam"* (Not unto us, O Lord, not unto us, but to your name give the glory). Hopefully, they will also see that the "not to us" of the first line is mirrored in the "but we" extol the Lord of the last line. In other words, the whole psalm, from beginning to end, is praise to the God who is in heaven. Congregation and clergy alike, and even a few converts, are all called upon to trust in this God, as well as be blessed.

Meanwhile, as Calvin once remarked, the human heart is an idol factory. Despite every encouragement to turn back, idolaters fashion images like themselves and mock those who have none. "Where is your God?" they say. But just because we choose not to make God as an image does not mean he is less real. On the contrary, the God of heaven is the most real thing there is, whereas those who make images are as lifeless as the things they have made. Without God they will simply depart to the realm of silence, whereas the earth will flourish in the fear of the Lord.

Prayer: *Keep me from idols, Lord. Keep me in your eternal love. Amen.*

Psalm 116
Individual Psalm of Thanksgiving

¹² What shall I return to the LORD
    for all his goodness to me?
¹³ I will lift up the cup of salvation
    and call on the name of the LORD.
¹⁴ I will fulfill my vows to the LORD
    in the presence of all his people.
¹⁵ Precious in the sight of the LORD
    is the death of his faithful servants.

PSALM 116 ASKS FAMOUSLY if there is anything we can do to repay the Lord, to which the answer is a resounding "No." The completeness of salvation means that our efforts are superfluous. But that does not mean we are thereby reduced to a life of passivity. On the contrary, as recipients of the grace of God we are called to the noblest task of all which is to lift up the cup of salvation, offer thanks to God in worship, and fulfill our vows in a life of obedience. As far as *contributing to* our salvation, these things add nothing; as far as *participating in* our salvation, they mean everything. In certain Christian traditions the lifting up of the cup in the Eucharist is the very heart of worship for here you have the perfect conjunction of praise and obedience.

Psalm 116 is often quoted at funerals, for obvious reasons. But in actual fact, it is precisely because the death of his saints is so precious to him that God ends up healing this supplicant. In other words, Psalm 116 is not a lament but a psalm of thanksgiving, and rightly takes its place as the fourth of the so-called Egyptian Hallel Psalms (i.e., Psalms 113–18).

Prayer: *Dear Lord, may my life be a constant lifting up of thanksgiving and praise for all you have done for me. Amen.*

Psalm 117
General Hymn

¹ Praise the LORD, all you nations;
  extol him, all you peoples.
² For great is his love toward us,
  and the faithfulness of the LORD endures forever.
Praise the LORD.

THIS IS THE BRIEFEST of psalms—the shortest chapter in the whole of the Bible. It was easy to decide which verses to highlight at the top of the page, since there are only two to choose from. Nevertheless, for all its brevity it offers everything that we need to praise God. In a world of instability, it extols the steadfast love of God; in an age of fickleness it upholds the faithfulness of the Lord. In short, this psalm presents to us the very heart of who God is, such that we cannot but praise him. More than that, this psalm takes us beyond the borders of Israel to embrace the peoples of the world. For St. Paul, Psalm 117 finds its final destination point in the mission to the gentiles (Rom 15:11). As people from all nations come under the sound of the gospel, so this shortest of psalms resounds to its highest decibels.

Prayer: *Lord, thank you for the privilege of seeing the gospel reach all people of the earth. Amen.*

Psalm 118
Individual Psalm of Thanksgiving

¹⁹ Open for me the gates of the righteous;
   I will enter and give thanks to the LORD.
²⁰ This is the gate of the LORD
   through which the righteous may enter.
²¹ I will give you thanks, for you answered me;
   you have become my salvation.

IT IS ALMOST IMPOSSIBLE to pray Psalm 118 as a Christian without entering into the last week of Jesus' life. From the festive throng who welcomed him into the city on Palm Sunday, all the way to his rejection by the chief priests and elders, this psalm has been deeply woven into the passion story. Part of the reason for that, certainly in the case of Jesus' spectacular arrival in Jerusalem during Passover week, is that this is an entrance psalm, a liturgical hallelujah, celebrating the great exodus of God's people. It's no wonder that it was chanted by the people as they caught sight of the long-awaited deliverer.

Jesus, however, will disappoint. As the First World War poet Edward Shillito put it: "they rode, but thou did'st stumble to a throne." At the end of Passover week Jesus will be strung up like a lamb, crucified like any common criminal. But if we think this is the end, the Gospel writers remind us from this very same psalm that beyond suffering lies resurrection hope: "the stone the builders rejected has become the chief cornerstone."

Prayer: *Praise you, Lord, that you take the rejected of the earth and place them center stage. How wonderful to be caught up in the drama of your great redeeming love. Amen.*

Psalm 119

Wisdom

¹² Praise be to you, LORD;
    teach me your decrees.
¹³ With my lips I recount
    all the laws that come from your mouth.
¹⁴ I rejoice in following your statutes
    as one rejoices in great riches.
¹⁵ I meditate on your precepts
    and consider your ways.
¹⁶ I delight in your decrees;
    I will not neglect your word.

WHERE DOES ONE START? Psalm 119 is longest of all the psalms, by a mile! It is a comprehensive A-Z, constituting 176 verses of what some scholars regard as a somewhat uninteresting, even boring, ramble on the virtues of law. Still others lambast it as the epitome of narrow legalistic religion. In truth, it is neither. What we have here is Psalm 1 revisited: a celebration of the expansive life that flows out of fidelity to the word, compared to the destructive life that ensues from vain disregard. Not once in the psalm do we get a sense of duty or dull conformity to the law. Instead, we encounter a passionate desire to stay close to the God who is faithful and wants our lives to flourish. In fact, it is worth noting that Psalm 119 is referred to in Hebrew by its opening words: *Ashre temime derekh* ("happy are those whose way is perfect"). Need I say more? "Happy" says it all.

Prayer: *Dear Lord, help me to see the beauty of holiness and the joy that comes from hiding your word in my heart. Amen.*

Psalm 120
Individual Lament

⁵ Woe to me that I dwell in Meshek,
that I live among the tents of Kedar!
⁶ Too long have I lived
among those who hate peace.
⁷ I am for peace;
but when I speak, they are for war.

PSALM 120 IS THE first of a discreet little collection of prayers known as the Psalms of Ascent (Psalms 120–34). They are all about making one's way to the presence of God, and likely were sung by the pilgrims as they made their way up to Jerusalem. This opening psalm is set far away in a strange land, among strange tribal people. Meshek and Kedar are almost mythical in meaning as places of hatred and violence. The disappointment we feel is almost palpable. Here we are hoping for a song of peace; instead we get a cry of war. But what this short psalm teaches us is that the first step back toward home, toward the warmth of the sanctuary, is only taken when profound disillusionment sets in. In other words, if we didn't feel the distress of living in exile, the dislocation of living among people for whom lies and deceit are second nature, it is unlikely that we would begin the journey home. Hence, the first note of the gospel is repentance: rethinking everything we have ever known, turning round, and heading back toward God.

Prayer: *It occurs to me now, Lord, that it was you who made me feel the emptiness of exile in order to bring me home. May I ever live in your peace. Amen.*

Psalm 121

Trust Psalm

¹ I lift up my eyes to the mountains—
  where does my help come from?
² My help comes from the LORD,
  the Maker of heaven and earth.

LIKE PSALM 23, PSALM 121 has worked its way deep into the affections of the faithful. "I lift my eyes to the mountains" has entered into religious language as a synonym for prayer and trust. Surprisingly, however, the mountains in this psalm are not a source of inspiration at all, but a threat of danger. Lurking in those dark defiles are bandits, thieves, and wild animals. And if that is not enough, there is the very real risk, as we make our way on pilgrimage, of getting sunstroke, being moonstruck, or stumbling over a stone. It will be a miracle if anyone makes it to the celestial city. Except that God is constantly awake and alert. He watches over us, keeps us under his shade, and guides our every step. As naive as it sounds, he watches over our comings and goings, now and forevermore. I look to the mountains and get nothing. In the end they are just mountains. I look *beyond* the mountains to the one who made the mountains, and my heart is strengthened.

Prayer: *Sometimes I wonder, Lord, where on earth I would be if you were not my keeper. What a privilege to have you watch over my every step. Amen.*

Psalm 122
Zion Psalm

[1] I rejoiced with those who said to me,
   "Let us go to the house of the LORD."
[2] Our feet are standing
   in your gates, Jerusalem.

THERE IS A STRAND within our tradition that sees personal silent retreat to some remote rural location as the epitome of the spiritual life. It has its place. Even Jesus withdrew at times to a lonely place in order to pray to his Father. Psalm 122 reminds us, however, that by far the dominant image of the spiritual life in the Bible is of a people exhorting each other to gather in the city for joyful worship. Such is the anticipation of coming together that the psalmist imagines he is already there, passing through the gates and into the courts of praise. But if we are thinking that pilgrimage is all about singing we are further reminded in this psalm that spirituality is also about justice, for the city is where the thrones of judgment stand, the supreme court in the land. The city is where everything is at, hence the desire to seek its welfare as well as its peace. As Robert Alter puts it in his translation: "Pray for Jerusalem's weal. May your lovers rest tranquil."

Prayer: *How wonderful it is, Lord, to gather together in worship. Is there any better place to be but among your people and under your peace? Amen.*

Psalm 123

Community Lament

¹ I lift up my eyes to you,
   to you who sit enthroned in heaven.
² As the eyes of slaves look to the hand of their master,
   as the eyes of a female slave look to the hand of her mistress,
so our eyes look to the LORD our God,
   till he shows us his mercy.

SERVITUDE AND FREEDOM ARE not words that we naturally couple together. In our world, slavery is oppression and freedom is release. However, this short affecting psalm celebrates a different kind of servitude—one that secures protection against an otherwise proud and contemptuous world. And it's not that we should presume on God. We are servants after all. But after years of watching and waiting, slave and slave girl alike have come to know that it is "always of his nature to show mercy." As they fix their eyes devotedly on the hand of the Lord, watching every gesture and movement, there is no cringing, no cowering in the corner waiting to be scolded, but only the thrilling expectation of grace. Not without reason it is called the psalm of the eyes.

Prayer: *Lord, even though it takes me a while to trust, I thank you that when I look to you I can expect only mercy and grace. Amen.*

Psalm 124
Community Psalm of Thanksgiving

⁶ Praise be to the LORD,
  who has not let us be torn by their teeth.
⁷ We have escaped like a bird
  from the fowler's snare;
the snare has been broken,
  and we have escaped.
⁸ Our help is in the name of the LORD,
  the Maker of heaven and earth.

THERE IS A DESPERATION that lies right at the heart of a life in God. Much to the disdain of the level-headed there is a glad admission among the faithful that unless God shows up we are ruined. To put it in the language of this pithy and poetic little psalm, if the Lord had not been on our side, we would have been swallowed alive—swept away.

For someone who sees life in altogether more reasonable terms, such language seems exaggerated—a bit melodramatic maybe. But for the rest of us mortals, for whom life can be overwhelming, the desperation is no more than is normal. And what it permits is insight and access to the most significant gospel truth of all: that God is indeed on our side, our help in times of trouble. Just as Israel escaped like a bird from the clutches of Sennacherib, so too will God deliver us from the snare of the fowler. For sure, we might wish it were otherwise. It would be nice to think we could control things a bit more. But we can't. We need help. And so it is that our experiences of life become a psalm of thanks, not a source of pride.

Prayer: *I don't mind admitting, Lord, that I need your help; and I can't help praising you, Lord, that you always deliver me. Amen.*

Psalm 125

Trust Psalm

¹ Those who trust in the LORD are like Mount Zion,
    which cannot be shaken but endures forever.
² As the mountains surround Jerusalem,
    so the LORD surrounds his people
    both now and forevermore.

THERE IS A FINE line between faith and presumption. Faith is when you look at the mountains that encircle Jerusalem and see it as a picture of God's protecting love. Wonderful. Nothing could be more thrilling than to know that God is with us in the pressures of life, defending us from disaster. As Spurgeon put it: "we are established and entrenched; settled and then sentinalled." Presumption, however, is when you think that the inviolability of the city—God's commitment to keep the marauders at bay—allows freedom to act as you want. Psalm 125 somehow speaks to both. It offers one of the most vivid images of assurance, of unconditional grace; yet, at the same time, it reminds us that the basin in which we live, where every provision is made to keep even temptation away, is also a place of demand. In other words, God is not to be trifled with. Hence, as we thank God for his grace, we remind ourselves to be steadfast.

Prayer: *Lord, since you don't let me be tempted beyond what I can bear, help me to trust in your encircling love. Amen.*

Psalm 126

Community Lament

⁴ Restore our fortunes, Lord,
  like streams in the Negev.
⁵ Those who sow with tears
  will reap with songs of joy.
⁶ Those who go out weeping,
  carrying seed to sow,
will return with songs of joy,
  carrying sheaves with them.

IT IS DIFFICULT TO know whether the first half of this psalm is past or future tense. It makes a difference. If past, then the prayer of part two is: "Do it again, Lord"; if future, then the prayer of part two is "Please God, make this dream a reality." Whichever way we go on this, the prayer nevertheless is just the same, and one we all recognize: the desire for God to send the rushing waters of renewal. And it's not that we resent hard work; nor that we don't expect to shed some tears. Let's face it, anything worth doing in life will exact a lot of emotional energy from us. But there comes a point when you expect a good return for your labor. After all, what's the point in sowing if you don't start reaping; and where is the solace in weeping when there's no sign of rejoicing—no hope of recovery? So yes, restore our fortunes, O Lord. Make those dry desert wadis transform into streams of living water. Make us laugh, make us sing.

Prayer: *Lord, we have spent many years sowing in tears. Now let us reap a harvest with unashamed joy. Amen.*

Psalm 127

Wisdom

¹ Unless the LORD builds the house,
    the builders labor in vain.
Unless the LORD watches over the city,
    the guards stand watch in vain.
² In vain you rise early
    and stay up late,
toiling for food to eat—
    for he grants sleep to those he loves.

IN A CULTURE THAT celebrates the self-made man or woman and which makes a virtue of busyness, Psalm 127 urges us have courage: to cut loose from the tyranny of a 24/7 world and simply trust that God can take care of our interests. Which is not to say we shouldn't work hard, but rather that without God it won't amount to much. In fact, praying this psalm teaches us an important irony: that if we try to burn the candle both ends we will become more and more anxious, whereas if we put God at the center, not only will we be more productive, we will also be at peace: for God gives sleep to his beloved, even as he gives to his beloved in their sleep.

So why does the psalm end with a celebration of sons? What's a full quiver got to do with our theme? Nothing really. Except that children are the supreme illustration of gift. We do nothing to earn children. We simply receive them as a blessing.

Prayer: *Oh that I would enjoy the sleep of the beloved: to be able to rest my head at night, Lord, knowing that you take care of everything. Amen.*

Psalm 128
Wisdom

¹ Blessed are all who fear the LORD,
   who walk in obedience to him.
² You will eat the fruit of your labor;
   blessings and prosperity will be yours.
³ Your wife will be like a fruitful vine
   within your house;
your children will be like olive shoots
   around your table.

EVERYONE WANTS TO BE happy. But not everyone is willing to wait for happiness. In fact, happiness has come to be seen as an entitlement as much as anything, with the result that it often seems to elude us. By way of contrast, Psalm 128 tutors us in the way of wisdom. It teaches us that the happy life comes to those who fear the Lord. By fear we don't mean snivelling before the Almighty, anxious that any moment he might fly off the handle, but rather what we might term reverent affection—a sense of awe concerning his majesty and grace. Furthermore, by happiness we don't mean adrenaline rushes, as we look for ever-new experiences, but the simple things like coming home from a good day's work, gathering around the table to eat together, laughter and joy as we recount the day's events, and a sense of hope and future. What could be more blessed than that?

Prayer: *Sometimes, Lord, when I look around my table, at the friends and family who are gathered there, I could cry with gratitude for the rich blessing that it is. Amen.*

Psalm 129
Community Psalm of Thanksgiving

¹ "They have greatly oppressed me from my youth,"
  let Israel say;
² "they have greatly oppressed me from my youth,
  but they have not gained the victory over me.
³ Plowmen have plowed my back
  and made their furrows long.
⁴ But the LORD is righteous;
  he has cut me free from the cords of the wicked."

IN THE PREVIOUS PSALM, we were singing about delightful blessings. Now in Psalm 129 the choirmaster would have us recount unbelievable sufferings—persecutions no less from the hands of our enemies. Contrary to what we might think, they don't contradict each other. On the journey to Jerusalem both blessing and suffering exist side by side. But if suffering is a reality for the people of God, the small print that maybe we didn't notice when we signed up to a life of faith, neither is it irredeemable. In a plethora of agricultural images, not only have the cords of the plough been cut, but those who have been driving the plough over our backs are now subject to the un-blessing of our prayers. Whether it is right to pray these kind of prayers is a big question. But there is surely a poetic justice in the fact that our persecutors might end up as withered grass on the rooftops, robbed of the joy of harvest.

Prayer: *Sometimes, Lord, it feels as if you have abandoned us, when all the while we are sitting on the edge of triumph. Help us not lose sight of your power and your justice. Amen.*

Psalm 130
Individual Lament

⁵ I wait for the LORD, my whole being waits,
  and in his word I put my hope.
⁶ I wait for the Lord
  more than watchmen wait for the morning,
  more than watchmen wait for the morning.

THE FIRST LINE OF this psalm is what makes it so loved as well as so memorable. This elemental cry from the depths—*de profundis*—assures us that there is no place too dark that we cannot pray to God, and no sin so sinful that God cannot reach us with his forgiveness. And it's not that we have to demonstrate reverence before God will forgive us. That is not what is taught here. Rather, we see that God's forgiveness of our sins inspires reverence and awe—as good news always does. No wonder, then, that the psalmist waits for the Lord. Such a promise of mercy, when all seems lost, inspires hope. Indeed, it generates longing. Not even the night watchmen peering into the darkness for the first sight of dawn can equal its intensity, for this is nothing less than the relief of God's redeeming word lifting the dark night of my soul.

Prayer: *O God, what security to know that no matter how dark things are I can cry to you and you hear me. Amen.*

Psalm 131

Trust Psalm

[1] My heart is not proud, LORD,
   my eyes are not haughty;
I do not concern myself with great matters
   or things too wonderful for me.

IN THE WORLD IN which we live, it is very easy for us to get ahead of ourselves—to aspire to things way beyond our reach. We are not helped by the fact that these days naked ambition is regarded as a virtue. By way of contrast, Psalm 131 is a maintenance psalm, pulling us back to the still center, urging us, as John Henry Newman once said, not "to see the distant scene, one step is enough for me."

It is the sort of psalm we should pray at regular intervals, for by it we cultivate not only a modest faith but also a mature faith: one that doesn't thrash around like an infant at the breast, always demanding something from God, but one that rests secure and satisfied in God's presence—like a weaned child. As a matter of fact, the Hebrew literally says "like a weaned babe I am with myself," thus giving us a beautiful depiction of prayer as a kind of self-containment. As strange as it sounds, in prayer I give myself the comfort and assurance a mother would give her child.

Prayer: *Lord, I am always concerning myself with things far beyond me. Today, I still and quiet my soul on your mothering love. Amen.*

Psalm 132

Royal

² He swore an oath to the LORD,
    he made a vow to the Mighty One of Jacob:
³ "I will not enter my house
    or go to my bed,
⁴ I will allow no sleep to my eyes
    or slumber to my eyelids,
⁵ till I find a place for the LORD,
    a dwelling for the Mighty One of Jacob."

FOR THOSE OF US who struggle along the way, trying to stay faithful to our call, there is great comfort in remembering that David's pilgrimage to Jerusalem was a journey full of torments too. The task of placing the ark in the temple exacted from him a great deal of emotional strain, not to mention sleepless nights. However, no sooner have we arrived with the psalmist in Jerusalem, we discover that for all sacrifices we have made in order to get there, and for all the promises to live dedicated lives, they are as nothing compared to the promises God has made to us concerning his anointed. Worship, we discover, is not ultimately what we do for God but what he does for us. As David finds out when the ark finally reaches its resting place, it is not for David to build a house for God, but for God to build a house for him. Christians of course rejoice in this every time they gather together in Jesus name.

Prayer: *Having arrived at your house through many dangers, toils, and snares, I don't want to miss out, Lord, on the sheer joy of singing praise to your name. Amen.*

Psalm 133
Wisdom

¹ How good and pleasant it is
    when God's people live together in unity!
² It is like precious oil poured on the head,
    running down on the beard,
running down on Aaron's beard,
    down on the collar of his robe.

ALMOST EVERYONE AGREES THAT community is a good thing. By it we are formed and sustained. This short psalm takes it further by showing us that life together is a spiritual thing, bestowing blessing from God. Two lush images are given to us, both wet with promise: luxuriant oil running down Aaron's beard and morning dew falling onto parched mountains. As we play with the sensuality in our prayerful imagination one suspects the psalmist wants us to experience something sacred coming down on us too—an anointing from God. Or maybe he simply wants to stir us to pray. After all, if unity is where the blessing is, then it would be surprising if somewhere along the way we didn't find ourselves praying the high priestly prayer of Jesus: "that all of them may be one, Father, just as you are in me and I am in you" (John 17:21).

Prayer: *Lord, help me to keep these gorgeous images before me, so that I will ever pray for unity. Amen.*

Psalm 134

General Hymn

¹ Praise the Lord, all you servants of the Lord
   who minister by night in the house of the Lord.
² Lift up your hands in the sanctuary
   and praise the Lord.
³ May the Lord bless you

We have come to the end of our journey—all the way from the darkness of the Bedouin tents (Psalm 120) to the darkness of the Jerusalem temple (Psalm 134)—a journey in fact of faith and anticipation because, as T. S. Eliot puts it, "the end is where we start from," the beginning of our ecstasy. Here in the temple, in the night hours, when all is quiet, when everyone has gone home, save those tending the fires, we lift up holy hands and bless the Lord. For the few of us left, these are the most precious hours. The darkness provides cover for the deepest kind of worship. And given that the Lord neither slumbers nor sleeps, this night vigil is as special to him as any large gathering. Maybe more so. Nevertheless, as we praise the Lord in this nocturnal assembly, we discover that our desire to bless the Lord, which has been the goal of our pilgrimage, is more than matched by his desire to bless us. The blessing returns so that the final words are benediction: not simply "Bless the Lord" but "May the Lord bless you from Zion, he who is the maker of heaven and earth."

Prayer: *I thank you that with you, Lord, darkness is not the despair of my sin anymore but the mystery of your presence. Amen.*

Psalm 135

General Hymn

¹⁵ The idols of the nations are silver and gold,
   made by human hands.
¹⁶ They have mouths, but cannot speak,
   eyes, but cannot see.
¹⁷ They have ears, but cannot hear,
   nor is there breath in their mouths.
¹⁸ Those who make them will be like them,
   and so will all who trust in them.

FAITH IN GOD CHANGES the way we see the world. And it's not that everything out there is bad, but it is hard not to be struck by how ridiculous things are. In comparison to the reality of the living, breathing God, imperious in his commands, devastating in his triumph over evil, the rest seems like a cartoon: puffed up idols that promise so much, glistening in silver and gold, but which have no breath at all. They are a pantheon of the deaf, the dumb, and the mute. Since those who worship them will be like them, then it is no wonder the world seems a lifeless place, whereas those who fear God are animated by the power of song. As Augustine once said: "a Christian is a Hallelujah from head to toe."

Prayer: *O Lord, thank you for delivering me from an empty way of life and giving me breath with which to sing your praise. Amen.*

Psalm 136
Community Psalm of Thanksgiving

¹ Give thanks to the LORD, for he is good.
His love endures forever.
² Give thanks to the God of gods.
His love endures forever.
³ Give thanks to the Lord of lords:
His love endures forever.

EVERY NOW AND THEN in the Psalter we are reminded that these psalms are set in the context of community singing. In other words, they are not so much personal prayers but corporate liturgies. Psalm 136 is a case in point, and like all good liturgies it opens up to the worshippers, by way of thanksgiving, the grand vistas of both creation and redemption. But whether it is the "brother sun" and "sister moon" of the Genesis creation, or the striking down and parting of the Exodus redemption, the thing that carries both is the enduring love of God. Through antiphonal response everything in fact becomes a window on the steadfast kindness of God, almost to the point of vain repetition. Or is it that by saying a thing often enough we actually start to believe it? Anyone who knows anything about good liturgy will know the latter to be the case. Try it. And see how love begins to grow.

Prayer: *How I love to join your people, Lord, in celebrating your creation and your redemption. We give thanks to you for your love endures forever. Amen.*

Psalm 137

Community Lament

⁴ How can we sing the songs of the LORD
 while in a foreign land?
⁵ If I forget you, Jerusalem,
 may my right hand forget its skill.
⁶ May my tongue cling to the roof of my mouth
 if I do not remember you,
 if I do not consider Jerusalem
 my highest joy.

EXILE IS SURELY ONE of the most traumatic experiences a human being can go through. Indeed, there is no other way to make sense of the end of this well-known psalm without reading it through the lens of what these days we would call post-traumatic stress. When you've been shamed, what else can you feel but vengeance? For all the loss, however, there is one thing your captors cannot take from you and that is the landscape of memory. No matter that we cannot rouse a song. No matter that we have had to hang our lyres on the poplars. It is possible to so internalize a place that even down by the rivers of Babylon we find ourselves remembering, maybe even motioning with our mouths, the songs we once sang. Though everything around us feels strange, in our hearts we are still home.

Prayer: *Thank you, Lord, that no matter how hostile and harrowing life is, nothing in this world can rob me of the joy that is in my heart. Amen.*

Psalm 138
Individual Psalm of Thanksgiving

⁶ Though the LORD is exalted, he looks kindly on the lowly;
  though lofty, he sees them from afar.
⁷ Though I walk in the midst of trouble,
  you preserve my life.
You stretch out your hand against the anger of my foes;
  with your right hand you save me.
⁸ The LORD will vindicate me;
  your love, LORD, endures forever—
  do not abandon the works of your hands.

HUMAN BEINGS ARE INCREDIBLY fragile—as fragile as pottery. If God, who is the potter, were to loosen his grip, we would smash into a thousand pieces. Hence, the prayer at the end of this psalm for God to "not let go of your handiwork" (Robert Alter's translation). It's an interesting prayer because the rest of the psalm has been a celebration of God's love and faithfulness. As we go through the psalm we recount a whole litany of wonders: when we call, God answers; even though God is on high he looks upon the lowly; he will bring me through "many dangers, toils, and snares," and ultimately God will requite me. Not for no reason Psalm 138 has been termed a psalm of thanksgiving. Such is our dependency, however, and our overwhelming sense of vulnerability, that even after all of that divine assurance it is good to remind God one more time that we are entirely in his hands.

Prayer: *Lord, I admit that for all your goodness, I still feel fragile. I join with the psalmist in praying that you keep your grip on me, gentle but firm. Amen.*

Psalm 139

General Hymn

⁷ Where can I go from your Spirit?
Where can I flee from your presence?
⁸ If I go up to the heavens, you are there;
if I make my bed in the depths, you are there.
⁹ If I rise on the wings of the dawn,
if I settle on the far side of the sea,
¹⁰ even there your hand will guide me,
your right hand will hold me fast.

PSALM 139 IS SURELY one of the most loved psalms. Heard hundreds of times at gravesides, bedsides, and chapels: and now, as we embrace it in private prayer, an anticipation of soulfulness every bit as introspective as a metaphysical poem. However, if we think this is all about the soul's quest to God, we are mistaken. To use St. Paul's language, this is not about knowing God so much as being known by God. This is about the Spirit's presence reaching us in the depths of hell, finding us on the far side of the sea. Whatever dark moods we may be passing through, praying this psalm assures us that there is light at the end of the tunnel; and that no matter how precarious life feels nothing can thwart what God has ordained for us.

No wonder the psalmist feels overwhelmed. Even the imprecations at the end make sense. For if God knows everything about me, knit me together in the womb, then he can surely take care of my detractors. The only thing he requires of me, it seems, is an open heart.

Prayer: *Lord, just when I thought I knew a few things, I realize that I haven't even begun to explore the mysteries of your all-knowing, all-embracing love. Amen.*

Psalm 140

Individual Lament

⁶ I say to the LORD, "You are my God."
  Hear, LORD, my cry for mercy.
⁷ Sovereign LORD, my strong deliverer,
  you shield my head in the day of battle.
⁸ Do not grant the wicked their desires, LORD;
  do not let their plans succeed.

THE WORDS "EVIL," "VIOLENT," "lips," and "wicked" in the first half of this lament are exactly mirrored in the second half of the psalm, in reverse order that is, thus creating an overall effect of unrelenting persecution against this faithful worshipper. And anyone who has faced such opposition will know that the malicious accusations can be as deadly as any physical violence. But if we think that persecution has the power to destroy faith, Psalm 140 reminds us that all it does is deepen prayer. The middle of the psalm in fact is testament to a faith forged in the fires of suffering: the essential I-Thou relationship that intensifies as the battle heats up. Indeed, such is the tenacity of faith that even when evil has done its very worst, we can still hope for justice of the sweetest kind because we know that God is on the side of the needy. Contrary to the old adage, justice delayed is not justice denied.

Prayer: *Lord, as I wait for you to carry out your justice in the earth, keep me safe in your mercy and strong in your love. Amen.*

Psalm 141

Individual Lament

³ Set a guard over my mouth, LORD;
   keep watch over the door of my lips.
⁴ Do not let my heart be drawn to what is evil
   so that I take part in wicked deeds
along with those who are evildoers;
   do not let me eat their delicacies.

YOU WOULD THINK THAT after so many years worshipping God, the sirens of this world would have less of an attraction for us. You would think that our faith could become so advanced that we wouldn't need to worry about sin and evil. Psalm 141 is here to warn us that this can never be the case. The temptation to collude with wickedness—evil words in particular—never goes away. In fact, the desire to answer slander with some invective of our own can be overpowering at times. Hence, the importance of keeping vigilant in prayer, as well as open to correction. It may not be pleasant. The rebuke of the righteous is hardly preferable to the delicacies of evildoers. But in the end it will keep us safe from the fate that awaits the wicked. As our Lord taught us to pray: "Lead us not into temptation, but deliver us from evil. For thine is the kingdom, the power and the glory."

Prayer: *However painful and however costly, I want to do whatever it takes, Lord, to stay faithful to you. Amen.*

Psalm 142
Individual Lament

³ When my spirit grows faint within me,
  it is you who watch over my way.
In the path where I walk
  people have hidden a snare for me.
⁴ Look and see, there is no one at my right hand;
  no one is concerned for me.
I have no refuge;
  no one cares for my life.

IT IS A SHOCKING realization—one that David arrives at in his desert cave—that in this life we are pretty much on our own. For all their best intentions, friends fail, promises are broken, and we find ourselves alone. We discover that the only person we can fully rely upon to watch over us and care for us is God. He is all we have—our portion in the land of the living. Actually, it's a wonderful revelation. Times of loneliness, like no other seasons in our lives, press us more deeply into God. Furthermore, knowing that only God can be trusted sets us free to enjoy people for who they really are, not for who we imagine them to be.

Notice that the psalm starts in lament, but it ends in gratitude. It begins in loneliness, but it ends in community. This community may not be everything we need. In fact, it can never be everything we need. There are no ideal places or people among whom we live our lives. But it's something. To be surrounded by the people of faith has its own comfort and its own reward.

Prayer: *I thank you, Lord, that just when I thought I was on my own, actually you are there right beside me, watching over all my ways. Amen.*

Psalm 143

Individual Lament

⁷ Answer me quickly, LORD;
    my spirit fails.
Do not hide your face from me
    or I will be like those who go down to the pit.
⁸ Let the morning bring me word of your unfailing love,
    for I have put my trust in you.
Show me the way I should go,
    for to you I entrust my life.

THERE ARE SOME FOR whom prayer is perfunctory—an exercise in felicitous speech; others for whom praying to God is a matter of life and death, in which case the language tends to be a bit extreme—ingratiating even. Psalm 143 is one such prayer, and by no means the only one in the Psalter, as we have discovered. No pretty phrases here, no emotional restraint as we seek to find the right words; rather, a full-on, honest cry that unless God shows his face I am lost. To those listening in who have never known such desperation, such praying can all seem a bit over the top. Why does faith have to be so dramatic? But for those who find themselves in dire straits, it is simply normal to pray this way. And what it affords is a corresponding intensity of relief when the darkness finally passes. When you have come through a night of despair, the morning ceases to be just morning but an announcement of love.

Prayer: *Lord, I don't mind admitting to you that I feel so desperate a lot of the time. Keep me ever dependent your love and faithfulness. Amen.*

Psalm 144

Royal

¹ Praise be to the LORD my Rock,
　　who trains my hands for war,
　　my fingers for battle.
² He is my loving God and my fortress,
　　my stronghold and my deliverer,
　my shield, in whom I take refuge,
　　who subdues peoples under me.

THIS PSALM MOVES FROM blessed at the beginning of the prayer to blessed at the end. In between is anything but blessedness. Instead we have a full-on fight of faith. As we advance, we notice that the skill of our fingers on the harp will be as important in the victory as the skill of our fingers on the bow. We will celebrate in song the triumph over our foes. Likewise, we will end up delighting in the beauty of our young, revelling in the abundance of our house. But if we are wondering where the power comes from to secure this victorious life the psalmist reminds us that it comes from God. With strong echoes of Psalm 8, as well as Psalm 18, we are led to ponder not the wonder of man but the weakness of man, and therefore our utter dependency on God. Personal pronouns abound to remind us that in the march toward peace God is everything: He is *my* rock, *my* fortress, *my* stronghold, *my* deliverer, and *my* shield.

Prayer: *I praise you, Lord, that you have brought me out of the shadows into the light of your glorious kingdom. I am truly blessed. Amen.*

Psalm 145

General Hymn

¹⁴ The LORD upholds all who fall
   and lifts up all who are bowed down.
¹⁵ The eyes of all look to you,
   and you give them their food at the proper time.
¹⁶ You open your hand
   and satisfy the desires of every living thing.

SCHOLARS TALK ABOUT PRAISE for who God is and thanks for what he has done. But since what God does is so much an expression of who he is, then the distinction is redundant. Yes, we praise God for his name is great. Indeed, Psalm 145 is "an overture to the last movement" of the Psalms, which is nothing but praise. But it's not a few verses into the psalm and already we are praising God for his wonderful works and his awesome deeds. In fact, we end up praising God for what we have repeatedly praised him for throughout the Psalter: namely, the way in which his greatness translates into compassion. In life it is usually otherwise. Might is right, and unyielding in its power. But in the kingdom of God, mightiness meets our lowliness and opens its hands in love. It does not despise our desire but satisfies it. All we have to do is look up.

Prayer: *Lord, it baffles me why so many people refuse to come to you in praise and worship. You are nothing but goodness and mercy. Amen.*

Psalm 146
General Hymn

³ Do not put your trust in princes,
in human beings, who cannot save.
⁴ When their spirit departs, they return to the ground;
on that very day their plans come to nothing.
⁵ Blessed are those whose help is the God of Jacob,
whose hope is in the LORD their God.

THERE ARE SOME PRETTY amazing people in the world. We are right to admire them. And who cannot fail to be impressed by pageants of princes and princesses. What we mustn't do, however, is idolise them, live our lives through them or put our trust in them. For all their beauty and vigor, they are human, after all. Like us, there will come a moment in time when they will take their last breath and return to the soil. Mere mortals, every one of them. But that doesn't mean we are bereft of heroes. Where princes cannot help, the God of Jacob can. He is faithful forever. The more desperate our plight, the more sure his aid, for he has "a preference for the poor." The sojourner, the widow, and the orphan all come under the purview of his special care, whilst the way of the wicked contorts. Psalm 146 is a sober but hopeful reminder that this is so. We will do well to pray it.

Prayer: *Lord, at a time when so many live their lives vicariously through the rich and the famous, I am going to live vicariously through you. Give me your heart for the poor. Amen.*

Psalm 147

General Hymn

² The LORD builds up Jerusalem;
  he gathers the exiles of Israel.
³ He heals the brokenhearted
  and binds up their wounds.
⁴ He determines the number of the stars
  and calls them each by name.
⁵ Great is our Lord and mighty in power;
  his understanding has no limit.
⁶ The LORD sustains the humble
  but casts the wicked to the ground.

WE LIVE IN A mechanistic universe. Pretty much everything can be explained by cause and effect. But if we imbibe this "cold philosophy" too long, to borrow a line from the poet John Keats, we will be reduced to dullness and impersonality. Psalm 147 is one huge antidote to that possibility. In praying it we become enchanted by love. In God's universe, the weak are not dispensed with but noticed and nurtured; the stars in the sky are not only numbered but named; and weather is not just weather but a sign of God's word. Indeed, poets speak of the divine scattering of the hoarfrost, meaning that this wintery landscape I behold, that I delight to walk in, is not to be explained by meteorology alone, but also by theology. Such a spiritual rendering of the weather may sound naive. In a world where might is right, where violence and virility are celebrated, it probably is naive. But then that is what living in the fear of God is all about: a return to innocence.

Prayer: *Lord, deliver me from this cold, impersonal world and open my eyes to the mystery of your creating and redeeming word. Amen.*

Psalm 148
Creation

¹ Praise the LORD.
Praise the LORD from the heavens;
   praise him in the heights above.
² Praise him, all his angels;
   praise him, all his heavenly hosts.
³ Praise him, sun and moon;
   praise him, all you shining stars.
⁴ Praise him, you highest heavens
   and you waters above the skies.

THE PSALTER BY DEFINITION is a book of praise. In this third of the five doxologies that bring the Psalter to a close (Psalms 146–50), a universal summons to praise is issued. Praise upon praise piles up, first from the heavens, then from the earth, until we are left with an overwhelming sense that everything in all creation is engaged in a celebration of God the King. It is not just the heavens but the highest heavens that are called to praise; not just the earth but the depths of the earth; and not just princes but all peoples: men and women, young and old. No stone is left unturned as praise moves through the psalm from the angelic host all the way down to the creepy-crawlies. And even if covenant is central to the story of God's purpose in the world, God is too majestic to be confined to borders. As St. Paul puts it in the great *Carmen Christi*: "at the name of Jesus every knee will bow in heaven and earth and under the earth" (Phil 2:10).

Prayer: *Lord, I feel giddy as I join with all creation in extolling your praise. It seems there is no part of this universe that is not full of your glory. Amen.*

Psalm 149

General Hymn

² Let Israel rejoice in their Maker;
    let the people of Zion be glad in their King.
³ Let them praise his name with dancing
    and make music to him with timbrel and harp.
⁴ For the LORD takes delight in his people;
    he crowns the humble with victory.
⁵ Let his faithful people rejoice in this honor
    and sing for joy on their beds.

WHO SAID THAT WORSHIP had to be solemn, or that saints had to be sour-faced? Psalm 149 shatters all our stereotypes by presenting us with a party that carries on late into the night. No half-measures here. No minor keys. Instead we have joyful singers, whirling dancers, and sword-wielding soldiers—even the odd tambourine or two—all gathered up in praise to the victory of God. If anything it all gets a bit over the top: a bit too triumphalistic maybe—even militaristic. But then again, why not? The world of the Psalms, as we now know, is a world of extremes. There is nothing moderate about them. The praise is as exuberant as the laments are deep. So it's no wonder, as we come to the end—and maybe as we are seeing the end with the final conquest of evil—that these are high praises that are in our mouths, just as it is a sharp double-edged sword in our hand.

Prayer: *Deliver me, Lord, from the mediocre middle and help me to praise with unapologetic abandon. Amen.*

Psalm 150
General Hymn

⁶ Let everything that has breath praise the LORD.
Praise the LORD.

THE PSALMS ARE LIKE an anatomy of the soul. In praying them we have given expression to a whole gamut of emotions. Indeed, it is precisely the rawness of them that makes them so universally appealing. But whatever emotions we have expressed along the way, here at the end of the Psalter everything gathers in praise. The praise doesn't cancel out the tears, any more than it fully resolves our questions. That would be dishonoring of everything that has gone before. Even so, we hold these things in suspense now as we gladly offer to God the sacrifice of praise. And what a noise we make. Like the roll call at the end of a concert, each section of the orchestra—wind, strings, and percussion—is summoned to play one more time, rising to a crescendo of clanging, clashing cymbals. We ourselves are enjoined to sing and dance. As the Chagall window at Chichester cathedral so colorfully paints: "Let everything that has breath, Praise the Lord."

Prayer: *Wow! What a crash, bang, wallop, with which to end these psalms. But it reminds me that whatever journey we have been on, all in the end is praise. Hallelujah, Amen.*